Russian
Festive Cooking

SUSAN WARD

A QUINTET BOOK

ISBN: 0–7858–0502–8

This book was designed and produced by
Quintet Publishing Limited

Creative Director: Peter Bridgewater
Art Director: Ian Hunt
Designer: Annie Moss
Artwork: Danny McBride
Editor: Barbara Fuller
Jacket Design: Nik Morley

Typeset in Great Britain by
Central Southern Typesetters, Eastbourne

Produced in Australia by Griffin Colour

Published by Chartwell Books
A Division of Book Sales, Inc.
P.O. Box 7100
Edison, New Jersey 08818–7100

Contents

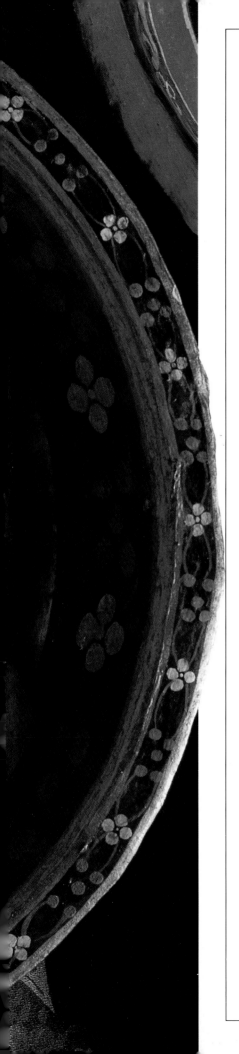

INTRODUCTION

'DOBRO POZHALOVAT' – 'WELCOME AND GOODWILL'. THERE CAN BE NO BETTER INVITATION TO THESE PAGES THAN THE TRADITIONAL GREETING TO ANY VISITOR CROSSING THE THRESHOLD OF A RUSSIAN HOME. FOR THE RUSSIANS – INDEED ALL THE PEOPLES OF THE OLD RUSSIAN EMPIRE – ARE INTENSELY HOSPITABLE, A TRAIT FOSTERED BY BOTH GEOGRAPHY AND RELIGION. OUTSIDE THE CITIES, DISTANCES ARE GREAT, AND OFTEN MADE MORE DAUNTING BY INCLEMENT WEATHER, WHETHER THE ICE OF WINTER OR THE BEATING SUN OF SUMMER. IN SUCH PARTS OF THE WORLD TRAVELLERS TEND TO BE GIVEN SUCCOUR WITH A GENEROSITY UNKNOWN IN TAMER AND MORE POPULOUS REGIONS. AT THE SAME TIME, THE ORTHODOX CHURCH – WHICH HOLDS SWAY OVER THE MAJORITY OF THE OLD REPUBLICS – EMPHASIZES HOME AND CHRISTIAN FRIENDSHIP AS UNIFYING FACTORS IN THE COMMUNITY. THE MUSLIM CODE, AN IMPORTANT INFLUENCE IN SIX OF THE ASIAN REPUBLICS, PLACES SIMILAR IMPORTANCE ON HOME, HEARTH AND HOSPITALITY.

HERBS AND SPICES IN REGIONAL CUISINE

ALLSPICE (*pimient*)

The dried berries of the Jamaican pimento tree, combining the flavours of cinnamon, cloves and nutmeg, with perhaps a hint of pepper. Scandinavia is the world's major importer, followed closely by Russia and the western republics, which use large quantities in fish packing as well as in desserts, pastries and savoury dishes.

BASIL (*bazilik*)

Both the purple and green varieties are used in Caucasian cooking, giving a depth of flavour to meat dishes, marinades and salads.

CARAWAY (*t'meen*)

A relative of dill and fennel. The seeds are used to flavour pickles, fish, cabbage, sauerkraut, soup, pork dishes and some pastries.

CARDAMOM (*cardamon*)

The pods and seeds are used in international cooking; the seeds only are included in Russian, Balkan and Ukrainian pastries and pickles.

CINNAMON (*koritsa*)

True cinnamon is a native of Sri Lanka, the bark of the *Cinnamomum* tree, though the more bitter bark of Chinese species also goes by the name. It came to European Russia and the Baltic by way of the Levant and the southern empire and is much used in pastries and desserts.

CORIANDER (*koriandr*)

A herb which resembles flat-leaved parsley and is sometimes used interchangeably with it in Georgian and Armenian recipes, though it has a more dominant, pungent taste. Sprigs can be frozen or preserved in salt and oil, but do not dry successfully.

DILL (*ukrop*)

A popular herb in most East European and Scandinavian cookery. The seeds and, especially, the feathery leaves, have a distinctive sweet-sour flavour much liked for pickles, fish dishes and breads. Chopped dill leaves are also used as a garnish, for example for potatoes or sour cream.

GARLIC (*chesnock*)

Evidence suggests that this herb originated in Kirgizstan, and was brought to the northern Russian states by way of the Silk Road. It is much used in pickles and meat stews.

MARJORAM (*majoran*)

Used in Middle Eastern cooking, this herb has crept across the borders into savoury Caucasian dishes. A particular wild variety which does not grow outside the eastern Mediterranean region is much prized.

MINT (*myata*)

A herb ubiquitous in Caucasian and Central Asian cooking, added to tea, salads, many hot savoury dishes and fruit compotes, it marries particularly well with lamb and cucumber, both favoured ingredients.

NUTMEG (*muscatny oreckh*)

A native of the Moluccas in the East Indies, this hard seed of the tree *Myristica fragrans* came north to Russia and Eastern Europe via the Silk Road and then the Baltic ports.

PAPRIKA (*krasny perets*)

A powder ground from the ripened seed pod of the red sweet pepper. The most prized – and sweetest – variety is that known as Hungarian paprika. It is used occasionally in Russian and Ukrainian cooking.

PARSLEY (*petruska kudryavaya*)

Only the flat-leaved variety is used. It has a slightly more marked flavour than the curly strain more commonly found in the West.

SAVORY (*chabyor*)

An atypical member of the mint family, having a sweetly piquant flavour much appreciated in the Georgian kitchen, where it is used in meat stews and marinades.

TARRAGON (*polyn estragon*)

A variety of European wormwood grown for its delicately pungent leaves. It is particularly evident in French and in Georgian cookery; in the latter it complements fish and lamb dishes, as well as vegetables and salads.

SUGGESTED MENUS

A REGIONAL MEDLEY DINNER
Mushroom caviar *(Gribnoy ikra)*
with sour-cream rye rolls
(balabusky)
•
Veal and liver pâté with gherkins and radishes
(Pashtet iz tielyatiny)
(s ogurtsami i ryedisom)
•
Stuffed cabbage rolls
(Golubsty)
•
Sweet apple bread pudding with lemon sauce
(Sladky pudding z yaablokami i limonnoy podlivkoy)

A TRADITIONAL ZAKUSKA DRINKS PARTY
Flavoured vodkas and/or vodka cocktails
•
Uzbekistan sweet walnut brittle
(Sladkoye pyechenye iz gryetskikh orekhov po-Uzbeksky)
•
Miniature salmon and cabbage morsels
(Piroshki z Iososemi Kapustoy)
•
Marinated mushrooms
(Marinovannye Griby)
•
Steak tartare
(Myaso po-Tatarsky)
•
Kazakhstan lamb potato cakes
(Kartophelnye piroshki z baraninoy po-Kazakhsky)
•
Minsk-style eggs
(Jajka Minsky)
•
Deep fried herb and egg envelopes
(Gutap)

A PICNIC EAST OF THE CAUCASUS
Yoghurt soup with apricots and walnuts
(Sup iz yogurta z abricosami i gryetskimi orekhami)
•
Poor man's caviar with toasted pitta bread
(Baklazahannya Ikra)
•
Cold pheasant Georgian-style
(Phazan po-Gruzinsky)
•
Karabakh salad
(Salat po-Karabakhsky)
•
Dried fruit and nut tart
(Tort iz sushyonykh fruktor orekhov)

A HEARTY WINTER LUNCH
Moldovan potato-cheese soup
(Moldavsky sup iz syra i Kartophelya)
•
Siberian ravioli
(Pelmeni)
•
Whipped eggs and sugar
(Gogol-Mogol)
•
Sweet caraway cookies
(Cepumi)

A COLD SUMMER LUNCH PARTY
Raspberry soup
(Malinovyi sup)
•
Lithuanian cottage cheese bacon bread
(Litorsky tworozhny khleb z beconom)
•
Chicken and potato salad
(Salat Olivier)
•
Transcaucasian cabbage and mint salad
(Transcavkazsky salat iz kapusty z myatoy)
•
Uzbekistan sweet walnut brittle
•
Pickled watermelon rind
(Marinovannya arbuznaya korka)
•
Tea ice-cream with rum sauce
(Chainoye morozhennoye z romovoy podlivkoy)

A REGIONAL FISH DINNER
Clear fish consommé with quenelles
(Ukha z Katushkami)
•
Onion-and-mustard herrings
(Sipoli Mércé)
•
Sevan lake trout Yerevan-style
(Sevanskaya fovel po-Yerevansky)
•
Spinach and walnut purée
(Pkhala)
•
Oranges with spiced rum
(Apyelsing v romye z pryanostyami)

ASPARAGUS VEAL BROTH

BAGRATION

◆ ◆ ◆

**This elegant consommé was named for Prince
Bagration, the Georgian general felled by Napoleon's troops
at the Battle of Borodino, outside Moscow, in 1812.
Though the battle ended in a draw, it marked an important
moment in Russian nationalism, culminating in the French
emperor's ignominious retreat from the capital.**

SERVES 6

- 50 ml/2 fl oz sunflower oil
- 1.5 kg/3 lb veal trimmings
  and bones
- 2 large onions, finely
  chopped
- 2 large carrots, peeled
  and chopped
- 2 x 400 ml/14 fl oz cans
  of chicken consommé
- 2 bay leaves
- ½ tsp crumbled fresh
  thyme
- 3 egg whites
- salt and freshly ground
  white pepper
- 450 g/1 lb baby
  asparagus tips
- sour cream
- fresh dill sprigs

Heat the oil in a large saucepan. Add the veal trimmings and
bones and toss them in the oil over medium heat until
browned all over, about 15-20 minutes.

Add the chopped vegetables and continue to cook until they
are lightly coloured and softened. Add the chicken consommé, bay leaves and thyme, adding water, if necessary, to
cover the meat, bones and vegetables. Bring to the boil and
continue to cook vigorously for 15 minutes, skimming off the
scum that rises to the surface. Then reduce the heat, cover,
and simmer for 2 hours.

Allow the stock to cool slightly then strain it into a bowl,
pressing hard on the meat and vegetables to extract as much
juice a possible. Cover, cool and chill for at least 12 hours or
overnight.

Pour half the stock into containers and freeze for future
use. Of the remainder, pour 300 ml/½ pt into a large bowl and
the rest into a saucepan.

Beat the egg whites into the stock in the bowl. Bring the
stock in the saucepan to the boil then in a stream, pour into
the egg-white stock, beating all the while. Pour the combined
stock into the saucepan and bring to a simmer over moderate
heat, whisking constantly. When just simmering, reduce the
heat to low, stop stirring, and let the stock simmer uncovered
for 25 minutes.

Line a sieve with several layers of muslin or absorbent
kitchen paper and place over a clean saucepan. Slowly ladle
the stock and congealed egg whites into the sieve, trying to
disturb the whites as little as possible. The resultant
consommé should be clear and delicate, leaving the impurities
adhering to the whites in the sieve.

Place the strained stock over high heat. Season to taste with
salt and white pepper and bring to the boil. Add the asparagus
tips and cook for about 4 minutes. Divide the asparagus
between the bowls and ladle the consommé over it. Garnish
each serving with a dollop of sour cream and a fresh dill sprig.

MUSHROOM CAVIAR

GRIBNOY IKRA

◆ ◆ ◆

Eastern Europeans, particularly Russians and Poles, are mushroom fanatics. Dawn expeditions into the wooded countryside in search of fungi are a common sight in autumn.

SERVES 8–10

- 350 g/12 oz fresh mushrooms (the more varieties, the better – field, shiitake, oyster, girolle, etc), finely chopped
- 1 medium onion, finely chopped
- 100 g/4 oz butter
- 15 ml/1 tbsp dry sherry
- 75 g/3 oz curd cheese

- 75 g/3 oz full-fat cream cheese
- 50 g/2 oz fresh parsley finely chopped
- 25 g/ 1 oz fresh tarragon finely chopped
- 25 g/1 oz fresh marjoram, finely chopped

In a large frying pan, sauté the mushrooms and onion in the butter over medium heat, stirring often. When the mushrooms are browned and softened, add the sherry. Remove from the heat.

In a bowl, beat together the two cheeses and herbs. Stir in the mushrooms, onion and their juices. Beat the mixture with a wooden spoon until it is well combined. Spoon the pâté into a small crock, smooth, swirl the top and cover. Chill overnight or up to three days before serving with small rye rounds.

VEAL AND LIVER PÂTÉ

PASHTET IZ TIELYATINY

◆ ◆ ◆

Pashtet can be made with veal and liver, pork and liver, or just liver; it can be served plain, set in aspic or baked in pastry. This is a fairly simple recipe enlivened with dried mushrooms, a favourite Ukrainian ingredient.

SERVES 8

- 225 g/8 oz calves' liver, chopped
- 225 ml/8 fl oz milk
- 50 g/2 oz butter
- 225 g/8 oz streaky bacon, sliced
- 1 small onion, chopped
- 1 stick celery, chopped
- 1 small carrot, chopped
- 1 bay leaf
- 4 peppercorns
- 225 g/8 oz lean veal, chopped
- 225 ml/8 fl oz chicken consommé or stock
- 75 g/3 oz dried boletus or porcini mushrooms
- 2 slices stale white bread, crusts removed
- 2 small eggs
- pinch of allspice
- salt and freshly ground black pepper

In a bowl, soak the calves' liver in the milk for 1 hour. Drain thoroughly and discard the milk.

In a frying pan with a lid, melt the butter over medium heat and coarsely chop and fry 175 g/6 oz of the bacon for 3–4 minutes. Add the onion, celery, carrot, bay leaf, peppercorns and veal; toss to coat in the bacon fat and butter for a few minutes. Then pour over the chicken stock and add the dried mushrooms. Cover and simmer gently for 1 hour. Add the liver and cook for a further 30 minutes.

Remove from the heat. Strain the stock into a bowl and soak the bread in it for 5 minutes. Squeeze out as much moisture from the bread as possible and process in batches with the meat and vegetables in a blender or a processor fitted with a metal blade. As the mixture is ground up, transfer to a large bowl. With the hands, work in the eggs, allspice and salt and more pepper to taste.

Preheat the oven to 180°C/350°F/Gas Mark 4. Line a 9x5x3 in loaf tin with the remaining bacon. Pack in the meat mixture, smooth the top, and cover the tin with foil. Bake for 45–60 minutes, until the pâté is browned and a wooden cocktail stick inserted in it comes away clean. Cool, remove from the tin, then chill. Serve in thick slices with black bread and butter and pickled gherkins.

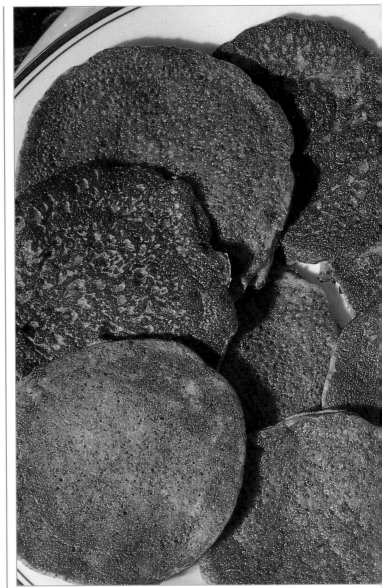

Buckwheat Crêpes with Caviar

BUCKWHEAT CREPES WITH CAVIAR

BLINI Z IKRA

◆ ◆ ◆

Leaving the batter for the *blinis* to stand overnight allows it to acquire its distinctive sour flavour. *Blinis* freeze well, and are delicious paired with smoked salmon or smoked meats such as ham and turkey and with cottage cheese accompanied by dried or fresh soft fruits.

SERVES 8–10

- ◆ *90 ml/3 fl oz lukewarm water*
- ◆ *2¹/₂ tsp (8 g/¹/₄ oz packet) active dry yeast*
- ◆ *2 tbsp sugar*
- ◆ *450 ml/16 fl oz milk*
- ◆ *225 g/8 oz unsalted butter, melted*
- ◆ *100 g/4 oz buckwheat flour*

- ◆ *100 g/4 oz plain flour*
- ◆ *1 tsp salt*
- ◆ *2 large eggs, separated, at room temperature*
- ◆ *175 ml/6 fl oz sour cream*
- ◆ *225 g/8 oz black caviar or lumpfish roe*
- ◆ *225 g/8 oz golden or red salmon roe*

Pour the lukewarm water into a small bowl. Sprinkle the yeast and ¹/₂ tbsp sugar over it and leave for 3 minutes. Stir to dissolve completely, then set in a warm spot for another five minutes, until it is foamy and doubled in volume.

Heat 225 ml/8 fl oz milk to lukewarm and stir into the yeast mixture together with the remaining sugar and 25 g/1 oz butter. Beat in the buckwheat flour for about 1¹/₂ minutes, then cover tightly with cling film and chill it overnight.

Next day, let the batter come to room temperature. Heat 225 ml/8 fl oz milk to lukewarm and stir into the batter together with the plain flour, salt, egg yolks and sour cream. Beat the mixture for about 1 minute, then cover and leave to rise for 1 hour or until foamy and double in size. In a metal bowl, beat the egg whites to stiff peaks. Fold them gently into the batter.

Place a griddle or a shallow frying pan over medium heat and, when it is hot, brush lightly with butter. Drop about 30 ml/2 tbsp batter on to the griddle so that it spreads into a 7.5–10 cm/3–4 in circle. Repeat twice and fry the blinis for 2 minutes, or until the undersides are golden. Brush the tops lightly with melted butter and turn them over to cook for 1 more minute. Repeat until all the batter is used up, meanwhile keeping the blinis warm, covered with foil, in the oven set at 120°C/250°F/Gas Mark ¹/₂. (The blinis may be made up to 2 days before and kept covered and chilled. Reheat in a 180°C/350°F/Gas Mark 4 oven for 15 minutes.)

Serve the warm blinis wrapped in a napkin on a heated platter, accompanied by pots of the caviar and roe in ice and an attractive arrangement of sour cream, finely chopped hard-boiled egg, sliced lemon and snipped dill.

ZAKUSKI

EGGS À LA RUSSE

YAITSA PO-RUSSKI

◆ ◆ ◆

While the origins of this dish lie within the borders of the Austro-Hungarian rather than the Russian Empire – it was a favourite of turn-of-the-century Viennese chefs – the marriage of ingredients justifies the name they gave it.

SERVES 6

- 6 hard-boiled eggs, halved
- 30 ml/2 tbsp mayonnaise
- ¹/₂ tsp dry mustard powder
- 15 ml/1 tbsp Dijon mustard
- 3 tbsp finely chopped sour-sweet gherkins
- 2 tsp finely chopped spring onion
- salt and freshly ground black pepper

To garnish
- capers
- paprika

Remove the yolks from the halved eggs, reserving the whites, and place them in a small bowl. Mash them thoroughly, then blend the mayonnaise, the two mustards, the chopped gherkins, spring onion and seasoning to taste. Spoon the mixture into the egg-white halves and garnish decoratively with the capers and paprika.

CHICKEN LIVERS IN MADEIRA SAUCE

PYECHYEN KUR V MADERE

◆ ◆ ◆

Served on its own, this recipe is a classic *zakuska*. but it is so delicious – and so rich – that it would make an elegant and inexpensive main course. Spoon it over rice or, more authentically, use to fill dinner-sized vol-au-vents.

SERVES 4–6

- *675 g/1¹/₂ lb chicken livers*
- *milk*
- *50 g/2 oz butter*
- *1 onion, sliced*
- *salt and freshly ground black pepper*
- *100 g/4 oz flour*
- *175 ml/6 fl oz chicken stock*
- *100 ml/4 fl oz Madeira*
- *90 ml/3¹/₂ fl oz sour cream*
- *fresh parsley, finely chopped*

Immerse the chicken livers in milk to just cover and soak for 2 hours. Drain thoroughly and discard the milk.

Melt the butter over medium heat and sauté the onion until softened. Dip the chicken livers in seasoned flour and add to the onions. Fry gently until just coloured, about 5 minutes. Stir in the stock and the Madeira, cover, and simmer for about 10 minutes, or until the livers are tender. Season the sauce to taste.

Transfer the livers to a bowl; boil the sauce until it is well reduced. Turn down the heat and whisk in the sour cream, a little at a time. Return the livers to the pan, spoon the sauce over and heat through gently. Serve immediately, sprinkled with fresh parsley.

CHICKEN OR VEAL AND PORK CUTLETS

KOTLETY POJARSKI

◆ ◆ ◆

These patties are encountered all over Russia in varying degrees of digestibility – from execrable to excellent. The latter are frequently served with the sauce given below.

SERVES 6

- *675 g/1¹/₂ lb minced chicken or mixture of 350 g/12 oz each veal and pork,well-chilled*
- *175 g/6 oz fine fresh breadcrumbs*
- *75 g/3 oz unsalted butter, softened*
- *100 ml/4 fl oz double cream*
- *large pinch of nutmeg*
- *salt and freshly ground black pepper*
- *2 large eggs, beaten*
- *30 ml/2 tbsp vegetable oil*

For the sauce
- *50 g/2 oz unsalted butter*
- *1 small onion, chopped*
- *225 ml/8 fl oz dry white wine*
- *225 ml/8 fl oz chicken or beef stock*
- *2 tsp flour*
- *15 ml/1 tbsp Dijon-style mustard*
- *30 ml/2 tbsp fresh lemon juice or sour cream*

In a blender or a food processor, combine the minced meat with 50 g/2 oz breadcrumbs, 50 g/2 oz butter, the cream, nutmeg and salt and pepper to taste. Process until the mixture reaches the consistency of paste. Remove, form into 6 cutlet-shaped patties, and place on greaseproof paper. Chill for at least 2 hours.

Meanwhile, start the sauce. In a stainless steel or enamel saucepan, melt 45 g/1¹/₂ oz butter and gently sauté the onion until it is softened. Stir in the white wine and the stock and bring to the boil. Reduce the heat and simmer, uncovered, for about 10 minutes, then set aside.

Using your fingers, knead the flour into the remaining butter to make a *beurre manié*. Increase the heat of the stock and drop in the *beurre manié* bit by bit, stirring all the time. When the sauce is thickened, remove from the heat.

Take the cutlets from the refrigerator. Place the beaten eggs in a shallow bowl and the remaining breadcrumbs on a plate. Dip each of the cutlets into the beaten egg, shaking off the excess, and then press into the breadcrumbs, coating each side well. Chill for another hour.

Heat the remaining butter and the oil in a large saucepan and fry the cutlets, 3 at a time, over medium-high heat for 4–5 minutes each side, or until golden-brown and cooked through. Remove and keep warm.

Finish the sauce by reheating it gently, stirring. Stir in the mustard and lemon juice or sour cream.

CHICKEN AND POTATO SALAD

SALAT OLIVIER

◆ ◆ ◆

A near relative of the 'Russian salad' so dear to the hearts of caterers and delicatessen owners, this real Russian salad is a traditional favourite, again refined and Frenchified by an imported chef. It would make a delicious main course for a summer luncheon or picnic.

SERVES 6

- 675 g/1¹/₂ lb cooked, boned and skinned chicken
- 5 hard-boiled eggs
- 225 g/8 oz new or small red potatoes, boiled in their skins and thinly sliced
- 100 g/4 oz cooked fresh or frozen peas, drained
- 2 large sour gherkins, finely chopped
- 175 ml/6 fl oz mayonnaise
- 100 ml/4 fl oz sour cream
- 10 ml/2 tsp Worcestershire sauce
- salt and freshly ground black pepper
- 100 g/4 oz black olives, halved
- 15 ml/1 tbsp chopped fresh dill
- 2 tbsp capers

Slice the chicken into 1 cm/¹/₂ in wide strips. Finely chop two of the eggs. Place the chicken and chopped eggs in a large bowl, together with the potatoes, peas and gherkins. In a smaller bowl, beat together the mayonnaise and the sour cream. Fold the Worcestershire sauce and half the dressing into the chicken mixture, seasoning to taste.

To serve in the Russian manner, mound the chicken salad in the centre of a large serving dish. Slice the remaining eggs and arrange the slices around the salad. Top each slice with a halved olive. Spoon the remaining dressing over the salad and scatter the chopped dill and capers over the top. Chill for 30 minutes before serving.

BEEF STROGANOFF

BEF STROGANOV

◆ ◆ ◆

The Stroganovs became one of the wealthiest members of the merchant aristocracy through their exploitation of Siberia's fur resources. The French chef of a late 19th-century Count Stroganov created this now internationally popular dish. It should *not* be served over rice – a heresy introduced by the West – but a tuft of straw potatoes on top is classically acceptable.

SERVES 6–8

- *1 tbsp dry mustard powder*
- *1 tbsp sugar*
- *90 ml/6 tbsp sunflower oil*
- *3 large onions, sliced*
- *450 g/1 lb fresh button or field mushrooms, sliced*
- *1.25 kg/2¹/₂ lb fresh beef fillet, cut into 1 cm/¹/₂ in wide strips*
- *salt and freshly ground black pepper*
- *600 ml/1 pt sour cream*
- *6 fresh parsley sprigs, stems removed, chopped*
- *deep-fried straw potatoes (optional)*

Combine the mustard and sugar in a bowl with water to make a paste. Let the flavours mingle while completing the recipe.

Heat half the sunflower oil in a large, heavy-bottomed shallow casserole. When just crackling, add the sliced onions, reduce the heat to low, and stir. Gently soften the onions, covered, for about 25 minutes, stirring occasionally. During the last 10 minutes, uncover and add the mushrooms. Remove from the heat, drain the mixture, and set aside in a bowl.

Heat the remaining oil in the casserole. Drop in half the meat, stirring with a wooden spoon and turning the strips over to brown evenly. Transfer with a slotted spoon to the bowl with the vegetables; sauté the remaining meat. When all is browned, return the meat and vegetables to the casserole, together with the mustard mixture. Season to taste and add the sour cream, a little at a time, stirring continuously. Cover the casserole, heat through gently for about 5 minutes, and serve. Top each serving with a light scattering of parsley, and the straw potatoes, if desired.

DESSERTS

TEA ICE CREAM WITH RUM SAUCE

CHAINOYE MOROZHENNOYE Z ROMOVOY PODLIVKOY

◆ ◆ ◆

This is an updated version of a dessert once served in the grand salons of Russian nobility. Elegant and light, it comes from the Silk Road through Central Asia and Caucasia

SERVES 8

- ◆ *100 g/4 oz kumquats, trimmed and finely chopped*
- ◆ *100 g/4 oz caster sugar*
- ◆ *30 ml/2 tbsp water*
- ◆ *2 tbsp shelled pistachios*
- ◆ *5 tbsp black tea leaves*
- ◆ *75 ml/3 fl oz boiling water*
- ◆ *5 large egg yolks*
- ◆ *350 ml/12 fl oz double cream*
- ◆ *3 large egg whites*
- ◆ *50 g/2 oz icing sugar*

For the topping

- ◆ *2 tbsp icing sugar*
- ◆ *15 ml/1 tbsp golden rum*
- ◆ *100 ml/4 fl oz cold double cream*

In a small saucepan, combine the kumquats with half the caster sugar and the water. Bring to the boil, stirring, then lower the heat and simmer, stirring frequently, until the kumquats are pulpy. Let the mixture cool and drain off the excess liquid.

Pour boiling water over the pistachios and leave for 1 minute. Drain and rub off the skins.

Place the boiling water in a bowl and add 2 tbsp tea leaves. Leave to stand for 3 minutes, then strain into another bowl. Press the leaves with a spoon to extract all the juice.

In a small saucepan, mix together the steeped tea and the remaining caster sugar. Bring to the boil and stir until the sugar is dissolved and the syrup is shiny and thickening, or measures 50°C/120°F on a sugar thermometer.

Meanwhile, beat the egg yolks in a bowl until they are thick and lemon-coloured. Pour in the tea syrup little by little, beating constantly, until the mixture has cooled.

In a saucepan, heat 100 ml/4 fl oz cream until it boils, remove from the heat and stir in the remaining tea leaves. Leave to stand for 5 minutes, then strain into a bowl, pressing hard with the back of a spoon to extract all the juice. Whisk together the tea-cream and the egg yolk mixture.

In another bowl, beat the egg whites until they reach soft peaks, then beat in the icing sugar until they become stiff. Fold the meringue into the tea-cream and egg yolk mixture.

In another bowl, beat the remaining cream until it reaches soft peak stage. Fold into the mixture with the pistachios.

Line a 1.25 litre/2¼ pt bombe mould with cling film. Spoon the drained kumquats into the bottom of the bombe mould, pressing up around the sides as far as they will go. Pour the tea-cream mixture into the mould and smooth the top. Freeze for at least 4 hours, or until it is solid.

Meanwhile, make the rum topping. Beat the rum and the sugar until the sugar has dissolved. Add the cream and continue to beat until the mixture has thickened. Serve the unmoulded ice cream with the rum sauce.

SOFT SWEET CHEESE PANCAKES

TVOROZHNIKI

◆ ◆ ◆

These hand-formed pancakes are sometimes served for breakfast in the better Moscow and St Petersburg hotels. The constituents bear a distinct resemblance to the fillings you will find in later chapters – the combination of lemon rind, eggs and cheese is a favourite throughout Eastern Europe and Western Russia.

SERVES 4–6

- ◆ *50 g/2 oz plain flour*
- ◆ *450 g/1 lb curd cheese*
- ◆ *1 large egg*
- ◆ *salt*
- ◆ *1 tbsp sugar*
- ◆ *½ tsp vanilla essence*
- ◆ *grated rind of 1 small lemon*
- ◆ *flour*
- ◆ *40–50 g/1½–2 oz butter*
- ◆ *sour cream (optional)*
- ◆ *fresh fruit – apricots, peaches, raspberries, as desired (optional)*

Sieve the flour into a large bowl, then force the curd cheese through the same sieve into the bowl. Add the egg, a pinch of salt, the sugar, vanilla essence and lemon rind. Stir to mix well.

Transfer the mixture to a floured board and form into 12 small patties. Arrange on a plate, cover with cling film, and chill for 2–24 hours.

Before cooking, dredge the patties in flour, brushing off the excess. Melt the butter in a frying pan and cook the *tvorzhniki* until they are golden brown on both sides. Serve warm with sour cream, and fresh soft fruit, peeled and sliced, if desired.

MEAT AND KVAS SOUP

OKROSHKA

◆ ◆ ◆

The kvas can be replaced by flat beer or semi-sweet cider, though the slightly sour flavour of rye will be missing. This dish may be served hot or cold.

SERVES 6–8

- ◆ *2 hard boiled eggs, separated*
- ◆ *2 tsp dry mustard powder*
- ◆ *150 ml/¼ pt sour cream*
- ◆ *salt and freshly ground black pepper*
- ◆ *1.25 litres/2¼ pt* kvas, *flat beer or cider*
- ◆ *1 medium cucumber, peeled, seeded and finely diced*
- ◆ *2 spring onions, including trimmed green top, finely chopped*
- ◆ *2 medium potatoes, cooked, peeled and finely diced*
- ◆ *225 g/8 oz cold cooked roast beef or pork, finely diced*
- ◆ *large pinch of cayenne pepper*
- ◆ *50 g/2 oz dill or chives, finely chopped*

Finely chop the whites of the eggs and set aside. In a bowl, mash the yolks with the dry mustard powder and a teaspoonful of the sour cream until you have a paste. Then slowly whip in the rest of the sour cream until smooth. Season with 1½–2 tsp salt and pepper to taste.

Whisk in the *kvas*, little by little, until the liquid is thoroughly combined with the sour cream mixture. Stir in the egg whites, cucumber, onions, potatoes, meat and cayenne pepper. Chill for 15 minutes, then ladle into bowls and garnish with chopped dill or chives.

CLASSIC BORSCH

◆ ◆ ◆

To most people borsch is the quintessential Russian dish. It appears in countless variations: clear and chilled for the summer, with a variety of meats in Ukrainian or Moldovan manner, or with the addition of less orthodox ingredients, such as mushrooms or barley.

SERVES 6

- ◆ *25–40 g/1–1^1/$_2$ oz butter*
- ◆ *2 beef shins, cut into thin slices*
- ◆ *1 large onion, chopped*
- ◆ *1 medium turnip, chopped*
- ◆ *1 large carrot, sliced*
- ◆ *900 g/2 lb fresh beetroot, diced*
- ◆ *2 litres/3^1/$_2$ pt beef stock*
- ◆ *60 ml/4 tbsp red wine vinegar*
- ◆ *2 bay leaves*
- ◆ *1 tsp sugar*
- ◆ *salt and freshly ground black pepper*
- ◆ *5 sprigs fresh parsley*
- ◆ *5 sprigs fresh dill*
- ◆ *225 g/8 oz white cabbage, cored and shredded*
- ◆ *225 ml/8 fl oz sour cream*

In a large saucepan, melt the butter over medium heat and add the meat, onion, turnip and carrot. Cook briefly, tossing the meat and vegetables, for about 10 minutes, until the meat is browned and the vegetables softened and sweated. Stir in the beetroot and 225 ml/8 fl oz of the beef stock, the vinegar, bay leaves, sugar and seasoning to taste. The soup will need quite a bit of salt to bring out the flavour, so don't be too stingy; about 1^1/$_2$ tsp should be about right. Cover the pan and simmer the contents for 45 minutes.

Uncover the pan and add the parsley and dill, tied together, and the shredded cabbage, along with the rest of the beef stock. Bring to the boil, then cover and simmer for another 30 minutes.

Before serving, remove the bundle of herbs and the bay leaves. Stir the soup, breaking up the meat and mashing some of the vegetables for a thicker consistency. Serve the soup in warmed bowls and top each with a tablespoon of sour cream.

SOUR BREAD DRINK

KVAS

◆ ◆ ◆

Recipes for this vary slightly in how sweet they are. Start with this slightly tarter recipe and increase the amount of sugar if desired. This is sold by street vendors and taken as a cold drink with meals, but it will probably find more favour with British cooks as an ingredient for cold summer soups.

MAKES ABOUT 3 LITRES/5 PT

- ◆ *450 g/1 lb slightly stale black or dark rye bread*
- ◆ *3 litres/5 pt boiling water*
- ◆ *5 tsp/(2 x 8 g/^{1}/$_4$ oz packets) active dry yeast*
- ◆ *100 g/4 oz sugar*
- ◆ *45 ml/3 tbsp lukewarm water*
- ◆ *1 large sprig of mint*
- ◆ *sultanas or raisins*

Preheat the oven to 110°C/225°F/Gas Mark ^{1}/$_4$. Place the bread in the oven for about 1–1^1/$_2$ hours, or until it is very dry. *Do not let it burn.* Crumble the bread into a bowl and pour the boiling water over it. Cover with a tea towel and leave for at least 8 hours.

Line a fine sieve with muslin and strain the bread liquid through it into a large bowl, pressing the bread with a spoon to extract as much liquid as possible. Discard the bread.

Sprinkle the yeast and a large pinch of sugar over the lukewarm water and stir to dissolve completely. Set aside in a warm spot for about 10 minutes, or until the mixture is foamy and almost double in volume. Stir the yeast mixture, the rest of the sugar and the mint sprig into the bread water. Cover with a tea towel and set aside for another 8–12 hours.

Strain the liquid again through a muslin-lined sieve placed over a large bowl. Sterilize 5 x 600 ml/1 pt bottles – glass milk bottles will do nicely. Pour the liquid into each bottle until it is about two-thirds full, then drop 4–5 raisins or sultanas in. Cover the tops with cling film secured with a rubber band.

Place the bottles in a cool dark place for about 3 days, until the raisins/sultanas have risen to the top and the sediment sunk to the bottom. Carefully pour off the clear liquid into a bowl, leaving the sediment behind. Thoroughly clean the bottles, remove the raisins/sultanas from the *kvas*, and funnel it back into the bottles (there will be slightly less). Cork the bottles or cover with cling film and refrigerate until ready to use. This will keep for several weeks well-covered in the fridge.

SIBERIAN RAVIOLI

PELMENI

◆ ◆ ◆

Traditionally, *pelmeni* were made in the autumn, with the coming of the first snowfalls. They were frozen, uncooked, in the snow banks outside the house, and hacked off in chunks whenever needed. The fillings used off-cuts of meat, while the dough could be made with or without egg. For fish *pelmeni*, substitute halibut, bream or salmon for the meat, and butter mashed with two hard-boiled egg yolks for the pork fat.

MAKES ABOUT 65–70

◆ *225 g/8 oz plain flour*
◆ *salt*
◆ *1 large egg*
◆ *melted butter (optional)*
◆ *sour cream (optional)*

For the filling

◆ *175 g/6 oz minced lean beef*
◆ *100 g/4 oz minced lean pork*
◆ *50 g/2 oz minced pork fat*
◆ *1 large onion, finely chopped*
◆ *1 tsp salt*
◆ *freshly ground black pepper*

To make the filling, mix together all the filling ingredients in a large bowl. Set aside.

To make the dough, place the flour and salt in the bowl of a food processor fitted with the metal blade. With the motor running, add the egg, then as much water as is necessary for the dough to just begin to form a ball (about 30–60 ml/2–4 tbsp). Remove the dough to a floured surface. Knead for about 8 minutes or until smooth, flouring the surface as necessary to keep the dough from sticking. Form the dough back into a ball, flatten slightly, and chill it, wrapped in cling film, for about 2 hours.

To make the *pelmeni*, roll out the dough on a lightly floured surface until it is a rectangle about 3 mm/$^1/_8$ in thick. Insert your hands under the dough and begin stretching it by pulling it carefully over the backs of your hands. When it is very thin, spread it on a table. With a knife, trim it into a square or rectangle and cut out 7.5 cm/3 in rounds with a biscuit cutter or lid. Drop a scant 1 tsp of filling on one side of each round. Brush the circular edge all round with a little water and fold over the dough to form a half circle. Seal by pressing the edges with a fork. Wet both ends of the *pelmeni*, bring them round, and pinch together in the shape of an Italian tortellini. Arrange the *pelmeni* on a baking tray, cover with a tea towel, and freeze overnight. (The *pelmeni* may be kept frozen for up to 3 months.)

To cook the *pelmeni*, bring 2 litres/$3^1/_2$ pt water to the boil in a large saucepan. Drop the *pelmeni* in by the dozen, bring back to the boil and reduce to low. Simmer uncovered for about 10 minutes, or until they rise to the surface. Remove with a slotted spoon, drain thoroughly, and bring the water back to the boil. Repeat with the remaining *pelmeni*. Serve with melted butter or sour cream.

PRETZEL-SHAPED SWEET BREAD

KRENDEL

◆ ◆ ◆

This much-loved sweet bread makes a delicious accompaniment to tea drawn from a silver samovar. Given a more cake-like consistency with the addition of more flour and eggs, but retaining the same shape, it is also popular as the centrepiece for a birthday or name-day celebration.

MAKES 1 LOAF

◆ *45 ml/3 tbsp luke warm water*
◆ *$2^1/_2$ tsp (1 x 8 g/$^1/_4$ oz packet) active dry yeast*
◆ *3 tbsp plus 1 tsp sugar*
◆ *350 g/12 oz plain flour*
◆ *$^1/_2$ tsp salt*
◆ *50 g/2 oz unsalted butter*
◆ *50 g/2 oz slivered blanched almonds*
◆ *3 standard-size eggs*
◆ *100 ml/4 fl oz single cream*
◆ *2 tbsp icing sugar*

Place the lukewarm water in a small bowl and sprinkle in the yeast and 1 tsp sugar. Leave for 10 minutes to become foamy and almost double in volume.

Sift 300 g/11 oz of the flour, the remaining sugar and the salt into another bowl. Cut in the butter in small pieces, and work the mixture with your hands until it becomes crumbly. Lightly beat 2 eggs and stir into the flour mixture, followed by the cream and the yeast mixture. Combine thoroughly to make a dough. If the dough is not firm enough sift in the remaining flour, little by little, until the dough is manageable.

Gather the dough into a ball and transfer to a well-floured surface. Knead for about 5 minutes, or until it is smooth and elastic. Reshape into a ball, transfer to a lightly buttered bowl, turning to coat in the butter, cover with a tea towel, and let it rise for 30 minutes or until double in size.

Knock down the dough and, on a floured surface, shape it into a long rope about 5 cm/2 in diameter. Taper the ends and twist the dough over and under into a pretzel shape.

Preheat the oven to 200°C/400°F/Gas Mark 6. Transfer the dough to a buttered baking tray, cover again with the tea towel and leave to rise in a warm place until it has doubled in size, about 30 minutes. Brush with an egg wash made from beating the remaining egg with a little water, and sprinkle with the almonds.

Bake for 15 minutes then cover with foil and bake for 10–15 minutes more, until the top and almonds are golden. Transfer the bread to a rack and when cool, sprinkle with sifted icing sugar.

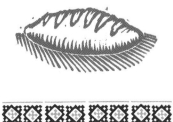

MEAT PATTIES WITH SAUCE

BITKI

◆ ◆ ◆

These tasty little patties can be made with either beef or pork – the latter is probably more common in western Russia and the Ukraine. While the recipe offers the option of cranberry jelly as an accompaniment, in its home regions *bitki* would more usually be paired with lingonberries.

SERVES 4–5

- ◆ 50 g/2 oz butter
- ◆ 1 medium onion, finely chopped
- ◆ 700 g/1¹/₂ lb lean minced pork or beef
- ◆ 225 g/8 oz lean minced veal
- ◆ 50 g/2 oz minced fresh pork fat
- ◆ 75 g/3 oz dry breadcrumbs
- ◆ 1 large egg, beaten
- ◆ salt and freshly ground black pepper
- ◆ 75 g/3 oz lard, chicken fat or dripping
- ◆ 150 ml/¹/₄ pt sour cream (optional)
- ◆ 100 ml/4 fl oz cranberry jelly (optional)

Heat the butter over medium heat and add the onions. Cook, stirring occasionally, until lightly coloured and softened, about 8 minutes. Transfer to a large bowl and add the minced meats, fat, 50 g/2 oz breadcrumbs, egg and seasoning to taste. Work with your hands until all the ingredients are well combined.

Form the *bitki* into 8–10 thick patties. Turn each of the patties over in the remaining breadcrumbs to coat them. Melt half the lard, chicken fat or dripping in a frying pan over high heat. Fry the patties until they are golden brown, about 5 minutes a side. Transfer to a serving dish and keep warm. Repeat with the remaining lard and patties.

Serve the *bitki* in either of two ways: sour cream can be stirred into the frying pan after the patties are finished, warmed through, and then poured over the *bitki*. Alternatively, serve the *bitki* plain, accompanied by a sauceboat of cranberry jelly.

RUSSIAN POTATO SALAD

KARTOPHELNY SALAT PO-RUSSKI

◆ ◆ ◆

This delicious salad incorporates the dressing which has now become internationally known as 'Russian Dressing'.

SERVES 6–8

- ◆ 900 g/2 lb new potatoes
- ◆ 2 tbsp finely chopped spring onion
- ◆ 3 tbsp finely chopped fresh dill
- ◆ 6 tbsp finely chopped sweet-sour gherkin
- ◆ 6 radishes, thinly sliced
- ◆ fresh dill sprigs

For the dressing

- ◆ 175 ml/6 fl oz mayonnaise
- ◆ ¹/₂ tsp Worcestershire sauce
- ◆ 23 ml/1¹/₂ tbsp ketchup
- ◆ 30 ml/2 tbsp dry white wine
- ◆ 5 ml/1 tsp horseradish sauce

Put the potatoes in a large saucepan of water and bring to the boil. Cover, lower the heat and simmer for about 20 – 25 minutes, or until the potatoes are done. Drain and when cool, cut into 5 mm/¹/₄ in slices.

In a small bowl, whisk together the ingredients for the dressing. In a large bowl, assemble the potatoes, onion, dill, gherkin and radishes. Pour the dressing over and toss gently to combine. Transfer the salad to a serving bowl and chill for 30 minutes before serving garnished with the dill sprigs.

FISH

Lake Fish in Mustard Sauce

Omul z Zaprvkoi Gorchichinoi

◆ ◆ ◆

Omul is a delicious relative of the salmon, found only in Siberia's Lake Baikal, one of the most beautiful lakes and on record as the deepest (1.6 km/1 mile) in the world. This recipe would use local wildflower honey and the fish would be baked over an open brushwood fire; here we must be content with ordinary honey, best Scottish salmon and a barbecue or grill.

SERVES 6

- ◆ *30 ml/2 tbsp sunflower oil*
- ◆ *1.5 kg/3 lb salmon fillet, washed and dried*
- ◆ *38 ml/2¹/₂ tbsp German-style mustard*
- ◆ *23 ml/1¹/₂ tbsp honey*
- ◆ *grated rind and juice of ¹/₂ small lemon*
- ◆ *1 tbsp finely chopped fresh dill*
- ◆ *salt and freshly ground black pepper*
- ◆ *dill sprigs*

If you are grilling the fish, brush a sheet of foil with a little sunflower oil before placing the salmon skin-side down on it. Whether grilling or barbecueing, place the fish (and foil, if used) on a baking tray. Mix together the remaining oil, mustard, honey, lemon rind and juice and chopped dill. Brush the fish liberally with the mixture.

Pre-heat a grill to hot. (If you are using a barbecue, the coals should be greying. Place the fish in a fish holder and turn it flesh-side down towards the coals.)

Grill or barbecue the fish about 13 cm/5 in from the heat for about 10 minutes, or until slightly translucent. Transfer to a serving platter and garnish with dill sprigs before serving.

STUFFED CABBAGE ROLLS

GOLUBTSY

◆ ◆ ◆

Cabbage rolls are made by Russians, Poles, Czechs and Hungarians, though each version has special spices and ingredients. The Hungarian one makes use of paprika, while typical recipes from the Ukraine – where they are called *holubsti* – contain mushrooms and are often meatless.

SERVES 8

- ◆ *1.25–1.5 kg/2¹/₂–3 lb white Dutch or Savoy cabbage*
- ◆ *40 g/1¹/₂ oz butter*
- ◆ *15 ml/1 tbsp oil*
- ◆ *2 large onions, finely chopped*
- ◆ *450 g/1 lb minced lean beef*
- ◆ *225 g/8 oz minced lean veal*
- ◆ *225 g/8 oz cooked long-grain white rice*
- ◆ *1 egg, beaten*
- ◆ *salt and freshly ground black pepper*
- ◆ *6 slices bacon*
- ◆ *400 g/14 oz can chopped tomatoes*
- ◆ *100 ml/4 fl oz beef stock*
- ◆ *1 tbsp flour*
- ◆ *150 ml/¹/₄ pt sour cream*
- ◆ *50 g/2 oz fresh dill, finely chopped*

Bring a large saucepan or casserole of water to boil. Lower in the whole head of cabbage. Cover and cook for about 8 minutes. Remove the cabbage but keep the water on the boil. Carefully remove as many leaves as you can without tearing them. Return the cabbage to the saucepan and cook for a little longer, then remove and again detach as many leaves as you can. Repeat the process until you have 20 or so large leaves. Trim each leaf, removing the toughest part of the central stalk. Set aside.

In a frying pan, heat the butter and oil and sauté the onion until it is softened and golden. Transfer to a large bowl and add the beef, veal, cooked rice, egg and seasoning to taste. Mix with your hands until thoroughly combined.

Lay 3–4 leaves out and place about 3 tbsp of filling on each. Roll up from the stalk end, turning in the sides, and finish at the leafy end to make a neat packet. If necessary, secure with a wooden cocktail stick. Place the packets seam-side down in a shallow casserole large enough to hold all the rolls in one layer. Lay the bacon slices over the rolls.

Preheat the oven to 180°C/350°F/Gas Mark 4. In a saucepan, heat together the chopped tomatoes and beef stock. Remove 30 ml/2 tbsp to mix with the flour in a bowl. Whisk in the sour cream and dill and return the mixture to the hot tomato-beef stock mixture, stirring. Season to taste and pour the sauce over the cabbage rolls.

Bake the rolls, uncovered, for 1 hour or until the sauce is bubbling and the rolls are slightly browned. Allow to rest for 10 minutes before serving.

HAM SAUSAGE WITH CABBAGE

KOLBASA Z KAPUSTOY

◆ ◆ ◆

Kolbasa is a smoked ham sausage common throughout the European states. Like many processed pork products, it is largely produced for sale in Poland and nearby Ukraine and Belorussia. It can be eaten hot or cold.

SERVES 4–6

- ◆ 1 large head red cabbage, shredded
- ◆ 25 g/1 oz butter
- ◆ 75 ml/3 fl oz lemon juice
- ◆ 100 ml/ 4 fl oz beef stock
- ◆ 50 ml/2 fl oz red wine
- ◆ salt and pepper
- ◆ 2 tsp brown sugar
- ◆ 1 tbsp cornflour
- ◆ 450 g/1 lb kolbasa or other smoked ham sausage, thinly sliced

Place the shredded cabbage in a colander and pour boiling water over it. Drain thoroughly.

Melt the butter in a heavy flameproof casserole over medium heat. Stir in the cabbage and sauté for 5 minutes. Add the lemon juice and continue stirring for another 5 minutes; the cabbage will be bright pink. Pour over the stock and wine, cover, and lower the heat. Simmer for 45 minutes.

Mix together the sugar and cornflour in a small bowl; stir in a little of the cooking liquid. Stir the mixture into the cabbage and raise the heat to high. Stir as the sauce thickens, then add the sausage. Cover and simmer for 30 minutes. Serve with thick slabs of rye bread.

HAM IN RYE PASTRY

OKOROK V RZHANOM TESTE

◆ ◆ ◆

This is a popular Easter dish which can be served either hot or cold, as here. It would be well partnered by cabbage cooked with sour cream, boiled potatoes with dill, and a pot of German-style mustard. The rather hard, dry pastry can be discarded before serving, if desired; it is really there to seal in the flavour of the spiced ham.

SERVES 10–12

- ◆ 75 g/3 oz dark brown sugar
- ◆ 1 tsp dry mustard powder
- ◆ $\frac{1}{4}$ tsp ground cloves
- ◆ large pinch of ground cinnamon
- ◆ 2.5 kg/5 lb canned Polish ham
- ◆ milk

For the pastry

- ◆ 2$\frac{1}{2}$ tsp (1 x 8 g/$\frac{1}{4}$ oz packet) active dry yeast
- ◆ 45 ml/3 tbsp lukewarm water
- ◆ 50 g/2 oz caraway seeds
- ◆ 75 ml/6 fl oz water
- ◆ 30 ml/2 tbsp molasses
- ◆ 375 g/12 oz rye flour

Make the pastry first. Dissolve the yeast in lukewarm water in a small bowl. Add the caraway seeds and set aside in a warm place for 10 minutes to become foamy and double in volume.

Stir in 175 ml/6 fl oz cold water, the molasses and half the flour, a little at a time. Take the resultant dough out of the bowl and place on a floured surface. Knead in the remaining flour, little by little. The dough should be stiff. Cover with cling film and set aside for 30 minutes. Meanwhile, remove the aspic from the ham and pat the ham dry with absorbent kitchen paper.

Roll out the dough to form a 66 x 25 cm/26 x 10 in rectangle. Mix together the sugar, mustard, cloves and cinnamon in a small bowl. Sprinkle a heaped tbsp of the mixture in the centre of the dough. Place the ham on top and pat the remaining mixture over the ham.

Preheat the oven to 180°C/350°F/Gas Mark 4. Fold the dough neatly over the ham, tucking the corners in and sealing it where the edges meet with a little water. Set the ham on a foil-lined baking tray, brush with milk, and bake for 1$\frac{3}{4}$–2 hours. Remove from the oven and allow to rest for 15 minutes before slicing the ham (and removing the pastry surround, if desired).

PASTRIES

SWEET POT-CHEESE TARTLETS

VATRUSHKI

◆ ◆ ◆

Vatrushki **are served as a savoury** *zakuska*, **as a sweet
to go with tea, as here, or as a large dessert tart.**

MAKES ABOUT 16 TARTLETS

- *200 g/7 oz plain flour*
- *$^1/_2$ tsp baking powder*
- *50 g /2 oz sugar*
- *pinch of salt*
- *1 large egg*
- *90 ml/3 fl oz sour cream*
- *65 g/2$^1/_2$ oz unsalted butter*

For the filling

- *50 ml/2 fl oz rum*
- *30ml/2tbsp water*
- *75 g/3 oz raisins*
- *500 g/18 oz cottage cheese*
- *4 eggs*
- *175 g/6 oz sugar*
- *2 tsp grated lemon rind*
- *100 g/4 oz clarified butter, melted*
- *$^1/_4$ tsp salt*
- *50 g/2 oz flour*

Make the filling first. Heat the rum and 30 ml /2 tbsp water in a saucepan over high heat until almost boiling. Remove from the heat and stir in the raisins. Set aside.

Line a colander with muslin and pour in the cottage cheese. Leave to drain for 3 hours.

In a large bowl, beat the cottage cheese using an electric mixer. Beat in the eggs, one at a time, and the sugar, until the mixture is pale in colour. Stir in the lemon rind, melted butter, salt and flour, 1 tbsp at a time. Drain the raisins, discard the liquid and fold the raisins into the cottage cheese.

To make the dough, sift the flour, baking powder, sugar and salt into a large bowl. Beat the egg and sour cream in a small bowl. Make a well in the centre of the flour and pour the egg mixture into it. With your hands, slowly work the flour into the liquid, then beat until the mixture forms a ball. Wrap in cling film and chill for 1 hour.

Preheat the oven to 200°C/400°F/Gas Mark 6. On a well floured surface, roll the dough out into a rectangle as thinly as possible. Cut out 16 or so 10 cm/4 in rounds from the dough, gathering and re-rolling the scraps as necessary. Make a rim around each circle by folding over and pinching up the dough, so that you end up with shallow tartlet cases.

Place the cases on a greased baking tray and spoon some of the filling into each case. Bake for 15–20 minutes, or until the *vatrushki* are golden. Remove and cool on a wire rack.

LITHUANIAN COTTAGE CHEESE BACON BREAD

LITOVSKY TWOROZHNY KHLEB Z BECONOM

◆ ◆ ◆

Varske – **cottage cheese – and honey are commonly used as a baking ingredient in Lithuania. This recipe mixes wholemeal and white flour to give a hint of the sturdier type of bread you will find in the Baltic States.**

MAKES 1 LOAF WEIGHT

- *50 ml/2 fl oz vegetable oil*
- *175 g/6 oz lean bacon, finely chopped*
- *2 heaped tbsp finely chopped spring onion*
- *50 ml/2 fl oz honey*
- *175 ml/6 fl oz milk*
- *1 egg*
- *175 g/ 6 oz cottage cheese*
- *150 g/5 oz wholewheat flour*
- *150 g/5 oz strong white flour*
- *2 tsp baking powder*
- *$\frac{1}{2}$ tsp baking soda*
- *scant tsp salt*

In a small saucepan, heat the vegetable oil over medium-high heat. Add the bacon and fry for a few minutes, until the bacon is cooked. Turn down the heat and stir in the spring onion, allowing it to wilt slightly. Then add the honey, heat through, and remove from the hob. Beat in the milk, egg, and then the cottage cheese. Blend thoroughly and set aside.

In a large bowl, sift together the two flours, baking powder and soda and the salt. Make a well and pour in the cottage cheese mixture, beating gently – do not overbeat.

Preheat the oven to 190°C/375°F/Gas Mark 5. Scrape the bread dough into a buttered and floured 9 x 5 x 3 in loaf tin. Flatten the top of the loaf with a spatula and drop the loaf sharply twice on a hard surface to eliminate air pockets. Bake for 45–50 minutes, or until the top is golden brown.

Place the tin on a wire rack to cool for 15 minutes before turning out. Cool completely before serving.

BARLEY BREAD

YACHMENNY KHLEB

◆ ◆ ◆

Barley bread is made from Finland to the Ukraine and it makes a change from the black and coarse rye breads which otherwise predominate in the countryside. In this Estonian recipe, honey is used to provide a touch of sweetness.

MAKES 2 ROUND LOAVES

- *$2\frac{1}{2}$ tsp (1 x 8 g/$\frac{1}{4}$ oz packet) active dry yeast*
- *50 ml/2 fl oz honey*
- *100 ml/4 fl oz lukewarm water*
- *350 g/12 oz cracked barley*
- *175 g/6 oz wholewheat flour*
- *2 tsp salt*
- *350 ml/12 fl oz lukewarm milk*
- *30 ml/2 tbsp vegetable oil*
- *175 g/12 oz strong white flour*
- *1 egg*
- *15 ml/1 tbsp water*

Dissolve the yeast, together with 15 ml/1 tbsp honey, in the lukewarm water in a small bowl. Cover the bowl and place it in a warm place for 20 minutes or until foamy and almost doubled in volume.

Meanwhile, in a blender or food processor fitted with the metal blade, grind the barley in batches as finely as possible.

Transfer to a large bowl and add the wholewheat flour and salt. Slowly beat in the yeast mixture, the remaining honey, the lukewarm milk and the oil. Add as much of the white flour as is needed to make a soft, malleable dough. Remove the dough to a floured surface, and, adding a little more white flour all the time, knead until it is shiny and elastic, about 10 minutes. Remove to an oiled bowl, cover with a tea towel and allow to rise in a warm place for 1 hour, or until doubled in size.

Knock down the dough, knead for another 5 minutes and form into two round loaves. Place them on a lightly greased baking sheet and leave them, covered, for another hour, or until well risen.

Preheat the oven to 200°C/400°F/Gas Mark 6. Make an egg wash by beating the egg with the water. Brush the loaves with the wash, prick the tops with a fork and bake for 15 minutes. Lower the heat to 180°C/350°F/Gas Mark 4 and continue baking for a further 30–35 minutes, or until the loaves sound hollow when tapped on the bottom. Cool the bread on wire racks and serve with unsalted butter.

GRATED POTATO AND EGG PUDDING

KUGELIS

◆ ◆ ◆

This is perhaps Lithuania's best-known dish. It is often served with a scattering of separately fried onions on top, but that does seem to be gilding the lily.

SERVES 4–6

- ◆ 1 kg/2 lb baking potatoes, peeled and grated
- ◆ 1 tsp salt
- ◆ 2 small eggs
- ◆ 2 tbsp potato starch or plain flour
- ◆ $\frac{1}{2}$ tsp baking powder
- ◆ 30 ml/2 tbsp melted bacon fat
- ◆ 1 small onion, grated
- ◆ $\frac{1}{2}$ tsp caraway seed crushed
- ◆ $\frac{1}{4}$ tsp pepper
- ◆ 50 g/2 oz butter, melted

Toss the grated potatoes in a colander with the salt. Drain for 10 minutes then, with your hands, squeeze out as much liquid as possible and pat dry with absorbent kitchen paper.

Beat the eggs in a large bowl. Sift in the potato starch or flour and baking powder and stir in the bacon fat, grated onion, caraway seed and pepper. Add the potatoes and toss well to combine.

Preheat the oven to 180°C/350°F/Gas Mark 4. Transfer the potatoes to a greased baking dish, smooth top, and pour the melted butter over. Bake the potatoes for 35 minutes, then increase the heat to 200°C/400°F/Gas Mark 6 and bake for a further 20 minutes, or until the top is golden brown. Serve immediately.

MEAT AND MUSHROOM PATTIES IN SAUCE

KURZEMES

◆ ◆ ◆

This, together with *ligzdinas* – meatballs stuffed with hard-boiled eggs – is Latvia's best-known main course. Neither is a subtle dish, but they appeal to hearty appetites gained from working in the open air.

SERVES 6

- ◆ 30 ml/2 tbsp vegetable oil
- ◆ 25 g/1 oz butter
- ◆ 2 onions, finely chopped
- ◆ 100 g/4 oz mushrooms
- ◆ 225 g/8 oz minced pork
- ◆ 225 g/8 oz minced veal
- ◆ 100 g/4 oz minced ham
- ◆ 3 tbsp finely chopped fresh parsley
- ◆ $\frac{1}{4}$ tsp dried thyme
- ◆ salt and freshly ground black pepper
- ◆ 2 tbsp dry breadcrumbs
- ◆ 1 egg
- ◆ 175 ml/6 fl oz beef consommé or stock
- ◆ 150 ml/$\frac{1}{4}$ pt sour cream

Melt half the oil and butter in a frying pan over medium heat. Add the onions and sauté gently for about 6 minutes, or until they are just softened. With a slotted spoon, remove half the onions and set aside. Add the mushrooms to the pan and continue cooking until they are very limp and most of the liquid has disappeared from the pan.

In a bowl, combine the three meats with the parsley, thyme and salt and pepper to taste, and the mushrooms and onions from the pan. Use your hands to mix thoroughly, then add the breadcrumbs and egg and continue to combine well. Shape the mixture into 6 patties and flatten them.

Add the remaining oil and butter to the pan. Melt over medium-high heat and sauté the patties until the meat is browned on both sides, about 15 minutes. Pour over consommé or stock, together with the reserved onions, and cook over high heat until the liquid is reduced by half. Reduce the heat to low and remove the patties to a serving dish; keep warm. Stir the sour cream into the sauce and pour over the patties. Serve immediately.

ONION-AND-MUSTARD HERRINGS

SIPOLI MERCE

◆ ◆ ◆

Onions and mustard appear in combination with herring in several Baltic recipes; sometimes the fish is in the sauce, as in Lithuanian *silke cepts*. In this Latvian version, the marriage is a bit more subtle.

SERVES 4

- ◆ *675 g/1¹/₂ lb fresh small herring, gutted, head, backbone and bones removed, washed and patted dry*
- ◆ *8 tbsp rye flour*
- ◆ *50 g/2 oz unsalted butter*
- ◆ *1 medium red onion, peeled, sliced and separated into rings*
- ◆ *2 tbsp finely chopped parsley*
- ◆ *lemon quarters*

For the coating

- ◆ *60 ml/4 tbsp German-style mustard*
- ◆ *15 ml/1 tbsp French-style mustard*
- ◆ *3 small egg yolks*
- ◆ *75 ml/3 fl oz double cream*
- ◆ *salt and freshly ground black pepper*

To make the coating mixture, mix together the two mustards in a small bowl. Whisk in the egg yolks, one by one, then the cream. Season to taste and whisk lightly again.

Spread out one herring on a flat plate. Spoon a little of the coating over the inside of the fish, fold together, and brush the skin on both sides with the mixture. Push to one side of the plate and continue with each of the remaining fish. Use any remaining mixture to recoat the fish. Cover with foil and leave overnight in the refrigerator.

Spread the rye flour on a plate and dip each of the fish into it. Melt the butter in a large frying pan over medium heat. Fry the fish in batches, turning to cook both sides, until they are golden brown, about 6 minutes. Keep warm until all the fish are cooked.

Arrange the fish attractively on a serving dish, with the onion rings and parsley scattered over them. Serve garnished with lemon quarters.

BEETROOT AND TOPS WITH SWEET-SOUR DRESSING

SVYOKLA Z KISLO-SLADKOY PRIPRAVOY

◆ ◆ ◆

A Lithuanian treatment for beetroot. If the stalks and greens are unavailable, use half the dressing on the beetroot and reserve the rest; it can be used to dress a celery and potato salad or carrot salad.

SERVES 6

- ◆ *1.5 kg/2 lb small-to-medium fresh beetroot with tops*

For the dressing

- ◆ *1 tsp dry mustard powder*
- ◆ *3 tbsp sugar*
- ◆ *23 ml/1¹/₂ tbsp honey*
- ◆ *15 ml/1 tbsp fresh lemon juice*
- ◆ *100 ml/ 4 fl oz white wine vinegar*
- ◆ *large pinch of paprika*
- ◆ *1 tsp caraway seeds*
- ◆ *100 ml/4 fl oz vegetable oil*
- ◆ *2 tbsp finely chopped spring onion*

To make the dressing combine all the dressing ingredients except the oil and spring onion in a bowl or blender. Whisk or process until combined, then add the oil in a steady stream, whisking (or running the motor) until the dressing is emulsified. Stir in the spring onion and set aside.

Scrub the beetroot clean and cut off the greens to about 2.5 cm/1 in from the top. Put the beetroot in a large stainless steel or enamelled saucepan and cover with water. Place over high heat, cover and bring to the boil. Lower the heat and simmer for about 15 minutes or until tender. Drain, allow to cool slightly, and slip off the skins.

Trim the stalks from the leafy green tops; wash and drain both separately. Chop the stalks into small pieces, place in another large saucepan, and add just enough water in which to steam them. Bring to the boil, cover, and simmer for about 5 minutes. Meanwhile, shred the greens; add them to the stalks and continue to cook until the green are wilted, about 3 minutes. Drain the greens thoroughly.

Cut off, and discard, the top ends of the beetroot and cut the beetroot into thin slices. In a bowl, toss in half the dressing. In another bowl, place the drained stalks and greens and toss with the remainder of the dressing. Chill both in the refrigerator for at least 2 hours before serving.

Transfer to a serving dish with two compartments or, alternatively, arrange the greens in the centre of a serving plate and surround with the sliced beetroot.

POULTRY & MEAT

CABBAGE ROLL PIE

KAPUSTNY RULET

◆ ◆ ◆

This recipe gives stuffed cabbage rolls, that favourite East European dish, a distinct Estonian-Finnish twist, by burying the rolls under a layer of puffy yeast dough.

SERVES 6–8

- ◆ 100 g/4 oz pearl barley
- ◆ 1.5 kg/3 lb head white Dutch cabbage
- ◆ 30 ml/2 tbsp vegetable oil
- ◆ 1 onion, finely chopped
- ◆ 1 small red sweet pepper, cored, seeded and chopped
- ◆ 225 g/8 oz minced lean pork
- ◆ 225 g/8 oz minced veal
- ◆ 2 sweet-sour dill gherkins, chopped
- ◆ 275 ml/10 fl oz chicken or beef stock
- ◆ salt and freshly ground black pepper
- ◆ 25 g/1 oz butter
- ◆ 4 tsp flour
- ◆ 15 ml/1 tbsp tomato purée
- ◆ 150 ml/¼ pt sour cream
- ◆ ½ recipe sour-cream rye dough or 450 g/1 lb packet wholewheat bread dough
- ◆ 1 large egg

Fill a large saucepan with water. Bring to the boil, add the barley and lower the heat. Simmer, covered, until the barley is tender, about 30 minutes. Drain the barley thoroughly and reserve.

Meanwhile, soften and remove the cabbage leaves. Repeat the process until you have about 18 leaves. Cut out the toughest part of the central stem in each leaf. Set aside.

Heat the oil in a frying pan and stir in the onion. Sauté until limp, about 6 minutes. Add the pepper and cook for another 5 minutes, until that too is limp. Take the mixture off the heat. Transfer to a bowl and add the meat, chopped gherkins, 30 ml/2 tbsp stock and salt and pepper to taste. Use your hands to combine well and divide into as many portions as there are leaves. Put a portion at the stalk end of each leaf, tuck in the ends, and roll to make a neat packet. Place the cabbage rolls in a baking dish just large enough to hold them in one layer. Set aside.

Melt the butter in a saucepan. Stir in the flour and cook for 3 minutes, or until the mixture is smooth. Whisk in the remaining stock and tomato purée; continue until the sauce boils and thickens. Take the sauce off the heat and stir in the sour cream. Pour the hot sauce evenly over the cabbage rolls.

Roll the dough out to a rectangle just larger than the baking dish. Lay over the top of the cabbage rolls and tuck the edges in. Use a fork to pull the dough gently towards the rim of the dish, crimping it. Cover the pastry with a dampened tea towel and leave to rise in a warm place for 20 minutes, or until risen and puffed up.

Preheat the oven to 180°C/350°F/Gas Mark 4. Make an egg wash by lightly beating the egg with a little water. Brush the wash over the pastry and bake until golden brown, about 45 minutes.

PORK LOIN WITH APPLE PRESERVES

SVINOYE FILYE Z KONSERVIROVANNYMI YABLOKAMI

◆ ◆ ◆

The accompanying preserve for this dish must be made at least 3 days ahead of time; the meat should be marinated for 24 hours. Leftover cooked meat, topped with the apple chutney, makes a particularly good cold sandwich on rye bread.

SERVES 4

- ◆ 1 kg/2lb rolled pork loin
- ◆ 100 ml/4 fl oz lager

For the marinade

- ◆ 15 ml/1 tbsp honey
- ◆ 1 tbsp finely chopped fresh marjoram
- ◆ 1 tsp juniper berries, crushed
- ◆ 1 clove garlic, crushed
- ◆ ¼ tsp dried black peppercorns

For the preserve

- ◆ 75 ml/3 fl oz dry apple cider
- ◆ 175 g/6 oz light brown sugar
- ◆ 3 dessert apples, peeled, cored and chopped
- ◆ 1 small onion, finely chopped
- ◆ juice and rind of ½ lemon
- ◆ ½ red sweet pepper, cored, seeded and chopped
- ◆ 1 clove garlic, crushed and finely chopped
- ◆ 2 tbsp finely chopped fresh peeled ginger
- ◆ large pinch cayenne pepper
- ◆ ¼ tsp salt

Make the preserve first. Bring the cider and brown sugar to the boil in a large saucepan; stir until the sugar dissolves. Add the remaining ingredients and bring to the boil again. Reduce the heat and simmer, stirring occasionally, until the mixture is reduced to about 425 ml/¾ pt. Cool, then chill for at least 3 days before using. (The preserve may be kept for up to 2 weeks in the refrigerator.)

Place the marinade ingredients in a large plastic bag. Add the pork loin and roll it around in the bag to coat it. Tie the bag shut and place on a dish in a cool place. Turn it occasionally in the next 24 hours.

Preheat the oven to 190°C/375°F/Gas Mark 5. Decant the pork from the marinade and discard the marinade. Place the pork on a trivet over a baking tray and roast until the meat is done, about 50-55 minutes. Remove the meat to a dish and keep warm.

Skim the fat from the drippings in the tray and discard. Pour the lager into the tray and bring the boil over high heat, stirring the dripping into the lager. Reduce the liquid until thickened. Pour into a sauceboat and serve with the pork and preserves.

SWEET APPLE BREAD PUDDING WITH LEMON SAUCE

SLADKY PUDDING Z YABLOKAMI I LIMONNOY PODLIVKOY

◆ ◆ ◆

The valued apple makes another appearance in this Lithuanian dessert, the sugar addict's answer to the savoury Potato and Apple Pudding. Vanilla ice cream makes a yummy cold partner for this warm pudding, as do mashed and sugared cranberries.

SERVES 6–8

- *100 g/4 oz unsalted butter*
- *400 ml/14 fl oz milk*
- *100 g/4 oz light brown sugar*
- *6 slices stale white bread, crusts removed, cubed*
- *2 dessert apples, peeled, cored and sliced*
- *2 eggs*
- *50 ml/2 fl oz Greek- or Bulgarian-style yoghurt*
- *¹/₂ tsp vanilla essence*
- *dash of almond essence*
- *¹/₄ tsp ground allspice*
- *¹/₄ tsp salt*
- *75 g/3 oz dates, stoned and finely chopped*
- *5 tsp wheatgerm*

For the sauce

- *175 g/6 oz sugar*
- *2 tbsp cornflour*
- *300 ml/¹/₂ pt water*
- *45 g/1¹/₂ oz butter*
- *45 ml/3 tbsp fresh lemon juice*

Heat the butter, milk and sugar together in a saucepan over low heat until the butter has melted and the sugar has dissolved. Set aside.

Combine the bread cubes and apple slices in a baking pan that will take them in one layer. In a bowl, whisk together the eggs, yoghurt, vanilla and almond essences, the allspice and salt. Stir in the milk mixture and the dates.

Pour the liquid over the apples and bread and leave to soak for 10–15 minutes. Meanwhile, preheat the oven to 180°C/350°F/Gas Mark 4. Sprinkle the top of the pudding with the wheatgerm and bake for 40 minutes, or until puffy and golden brown.

Meanwhile, make the sauce. In a saucepan, stir the sugar and cornflour in the water over high heat until boiling. Add the butter and lemon juice, stirring, and when the butter is dissolved, remove from the heat.

Serve the apple bread pudding warm, accompanied by the warm lemon sauce.

BERRY DESSERT PANCAKES

PANNKOOGID

◆ ◆ ◆

These Estonian pancakes are huge – the size of plates – and have a fluffy consistency quite unlike the familiar pancake. In their native surroundings they would often be served with lingonberries – but raspberries or blueberries are just as scrumptious.

SERVES 6

- ◆ 100 g/4 oz plain flour
- ◆ 25 g/1 oz sugar
- ◆ pinch of salt
- ◆ 2 eggs, separated
- ◆ 225 ml/8 fl oz milk
- ◆ ¹/₂ tsp vanilla essence

For the filling

- ◆ 225/ 8 oz fresh raspberries or blueberries
- ◆ 30 ml/2 tbsp water
- ◆ 100 g/4 oz sugar
- ◆ 1 tbsp cornflour

Sift the flour, sugar and salt into a large bowl. Make a well in the centre. Drop the egg yolks, the milk and vanilla into the well, then beat to combine thoroughly with the flour. The batter will be thin. Cover it with a cloth and leave in a cool – not cold – place overnight to mature.

To make the filling, rinse and drain the berries and place in an enamelled or stainless steel saucepan, together with the water and the sugar. Cook over medium-high heat, stirring, until the berries are dissolving into a sauce, with some remaining whole. Bring to the boil, stir in the cornflour and reduce the heat. Cook for 5–10 minutes, stirring until the filling mixture has thickened. Remove from the heat, pour into an attractive bowl and allow to cool.

Before using the batter, beat the egg whites in a large bowl until they form stiff peaks. With a rubber or plastic spatula, carefully fold them into the batter.

Lightly coat a large non-stick crêpe or frying pan with butter and heat until medium-hot. Remove from the heat and pour in 100 ml/4 fl oz of the batter. Tilt the pan to spread it evenly, then replace on the heat and fry the pancake for about 3 minutes a side, until golden. Slide the pancake on to a dish and keep warm while you make the rest of the pancakes.

Serve each pancake flat on a plate, accompanied by the bowl of fruit sauce.

'ALMOST NOTHING' SOUP

POCHTY NICHEVO

◆ ◆ ◆

This soup, made from scraps, has a surprising flavour, smoky and nut-like. Add a little cream to make it more sophisticated.

SERVES 4 – 6

◆ *1.5 kg/3 lb beef, chicken, veal or mixed bones*
◆ *1 onion, unpeeled*
◆ *salt and freshly ground black pepper*
◆ *1.75 litres/3¼ pt water*
◆ *1 kg/2 lb potatoes, scrubbed and dried*
◆ *100ml/4oz bacon fat or melted butter*
◆ *100 ml/4 fl oz single cream (optional)*
◆ *2 tbsp chopped fresh chives*

Place the bones, the unpeeled onion and seasoning to taste in a large pot. Cover with the water and put over high heat. Bring to the boil, then cover and simmer for 1 hour. Uncover and continue to simmer until the stock has reduced to almost half. Strain the stock and return to the saucepan.

Meanwhile peel the potatoes. Reserve the potatoes themselves for another use. Melt the bacon fat or butter in a frying pan and sauté the onion until soft, about 6 minutes. Add the potato skins and continue to cook until they too are tender.

Transfer the potato skins and onion to the saucepan containing the stock. Bring to the boil, then reduce the heat and simmer for 10 minutes. Purée the soup in batches; return to the saucepan and reheat. Thin, if necessary, with a little water or the single cream. Ladle into individual bowls and serve sprinkled with the chopped chives.

GRILLED CORNMEAL CAKE WITH CHEESE

MAMALYGA

◆ ◆ ◆

Moldovan food exhibits a legacy of the days between the wars when it was a part of Romania, and of the generations before that when it had many unofficial links with that country. This polenta-like hard cake has a Balkan flavour; it is often served with *borsch* or cabbage dishes.

SERVES 6

- ◆ *150 g/5 oz stone-ground yellow cornmeal*
- ◆ *1 litre/1³/₄ pt water*
- ◆ *1–1¹/₂ tsp salt*
- ◆ *50 g/2 oz butter*
- ◆ *pinch of dried marjoram*

- ◆ *large pinch of cayenne pepper*
- ◆ *275 g/10 oz hard ewe's or goat's cheese, or Lancashire cheese*
- ◆ *salt and freshly ground black pepper*

Stir the cornmeal in a large frying pan over medium heat for 4 minutes, or until it loses its bright yellow colour and becomes light beige.

Pour the water into a saucepan. Put the hot cornmeal into the water, it should hiss; then stir in the salt to taste. Cook over moderate heat for 5 minutes, stirring, until the liquid begins to boil. Cover, lower the heat and simmer for 20 minutes, stirring frequently.

Preheat the oven to 190°C/375°F/Gas Mark 5. Uncover the saucepan and continue to stir until the polenta is very thick and the spoon is drawing it away from the bottom and sides of the pan. Remove from the heat, add the butter, marjoram and pepper, and stir until the butter is melted into the polenta. Stir in three-quarters of the cheese, then turn the polenta into a shallow buttered baking dish.

Bake for 40 minutes on the top shelf of the oven, until the cake has a skin over it. Remove from the oven and allow to cool and set for at least 1 hour. (The cake can be kept refrigerated for up to 3 days.)

To serve, heat the grill to hot. Slice the cake into squares or wedges and sprinkle over the remaining cheese. Grill until the cheesy crust is golden-brown and the *mamalyga* is hot. Serve immediately.

CHICKEN KIEV

KOTLETY PO-KIEVSKY

◆ ◆ ◆

Chicken Kiev has become a familiar dish, stacked frozen and ready-to-heat in supermarkets and frequently appearing on menus, even in pubs. But the real thing bears little resemblance, in appearance or taste, to such orange monstrosities. The recipe has been simplified to take advantage of prepared chicken breasts.

SERVES 6

- *150 g/6 oz unsalted butter, softened*
- *grated rind and juice of 1 large lemon*
- *3 tbsp freshly chopped tarragon*
- *6 large skinless chicken breast fillets*
- *salt and freshly ground black pepper*
- *2 small eggs*
- *175 g/6 oz fresh fine breadcrumbs*
- *oil for deep-frying*

Combine the butter, lemon rind and tarragon in a bowl. With a fork, work the mixture until it is thoroughly mixed. Shape into a block, wrap in foil, and chill until hard.

Lay the chicken breasts on a sheet of greaseproof paper.

Trim away any bits attached by membrane. Cover the breasts with another sheet of greaseproof paper and pound with a mallet until they are flattened. Season the fillets as desired.

Cut the butter block into 6 pieces and place one piece in the centre of each fillet. Fold the top and edges over, then roll neatly. Tie the roll with thread.

Beat the eggs lightly in a shallow bowl. Spread the breadcrumbs on a large plate. Dip the breast rolls in the egg then coat them in the breadcrumbs, pressing into the crumbs to make sure they adhere. To obtain a thick 'skin' brush the coated rolls with a little more egg if necessary and press into the crumbs again. Place the rolls on a plate and chill for 2–3 hours.

In a deep fryer or heavy saucepan, heat enough oil to cover the breasts completely. When it spits at water droplets (or reaches 190°/375°F), lower in 3 breasts with a slotted spoon. Fry until golden-brown, about 5–6 minutes. (The oil must not get too hot or the coating will brown before the chicken is cooked.) Drain on absorbent kitchen paper and repeat with the remaining 3 breasts. Serve immediately. Potatoes and cabbage or peas would make a typical accompaniment.

STEWED LAMB WITH MUSHROOMS AND BARLEY

TYSHYONAYA BARANINAZ GRIBAMI I YACHMENYOM

◆ ◆ ◆

This is a Moldovan dish, from the foothills of the Carpathian mountains. It is unsophisticated and hardly pretty-pretty, but it is nutritious, inexpensive and full-flavoured, a true rustic feast.

SERVES 6

- ◆ *1.25 kg/2$^{1}/_{2}$ lb shanks or neck of lamb, cut into pieces*
- ◆ *90 ml/ 3$^{1}/_{2}$ fl oz vegetable oil*
- ◆ *1 medium onion, chopped*
- ◆ *2 long red medium-hot peppers, seeded and chopped*
- ◆ *175 g/6 oz field or button mushrooms, wiped and sliced*
- ◆ *15 ml/1 tbsp German-style mustard*
- ◆ *700 ml/1$^{1}/_{4}$ pt chicken stock*
- ◆ *75 ml/3 fl oz white wine vinegar*
- ◆ *225 g/8 oz pearl barley*
- ◆ *1 tsp cumin seeds*
- ◆ *2 whole cloves*
- ◆ *2 tsp dried dill*
- ◆ *salt and freshly ground black pepper*
- ◆ *225 ml/8 fl oz sour cream or yoghurt*
- ◆ *50 g/2 oz flat-leaved parsley, finely chopped*

In a heavy casserole, brown the lamb shank or neck pieces in half the oil until they are coloured. Remove with a slotted spoon and set aside. Add the onion to the casserole, and cook until it is soft and lightly coloured, about 6–8 minutes. Remove with the slotted spoon and set aside. Add the rest of the oil and sauté the red peppers and mushroom for about 5 minutes, or until the mushrooms are softened. Remove to a bowl and set aside.

Preheat the oven to 170°C/325°F/Gas Mark 3. Stir the onions and lamb back into the casserole, together with the mustard. Add the chicken stock and the wine vinegar, bring to the boil, and transfer the casserole to the oven. Bake for 1$^{1}/_{2}$ hours, until the lamb is very tender and falling off the bones.

Remove the lamb from the casserole. Using your hands and a fork, pull the meat from the bones and chop it. Return to the casserole and stir into the stock with the barley, cumin seeds, cloves, dill and seasoning to taste. Bring to the boil, cover and lower the heat. Simmer for about 1 hour, until the barley is tender and most of the stock has been absorbed.

Stir the red pepper and mushrooms into the stew, together with the sour cream or yoghurt. Heat through for about 10–12 minutes, take off the heat, stir in the chopped parsley, and bring to the table to serve.

ONION, LENTIL AND LEMON SOUP
SUP IZ LUKA, GOROKHA I LIMONA
◆ ◆ ◆

Barley and lentils are two Armenian favourites paired in this earthy soup. Served with warm cornbread it would make a filling supper or lunch.

SERVES 6

- 225 ml/8 fl oz water
- 75 g/3 oz pearl barley
- 15 ml/1 tbsp tomato puree
- 1.5 litres/2^1/$_2$ pt beef stock
- 175 g/6 oz brown lentils, rinsed and picked over
- 5 onions, sliced very thinly
- 1 tsp dried anise seeds
- juice of 1 large lemon
- large pinch of sweet paprika
- pinch of cayenne pepper
- salt and freshly ground black pepper
- 12 paper-thin lemon slices

Bring the water to the boil in a large enamelled or stainless steel saucepan. Stir in the barley, cover, and simmer over low heat for about 20–25 minutes, until the barley is just tender and the water has been absorbed. Stir in the tomato purée, beef stock, lentils, onions and anise. Bring to the boil, cover, and simmer over low heat for 1 hour, or until the lentils are soft.

Stir in the lemon juice, paprika, cayenne pepper and salt and pepper to taste and simmer uncovered for a further 20 minutes. Pour the soup into heated bowls and garnish each with two very thin slices of lemon.

POOR MAN'S CAVIAR

BAKLAZHANNYA IKRA

◆ ◆ ◆

**The smoky flavour of this Georgian 'caviar' has
become familiar to Westerners through Lebanese and
Turkish restaurants which also serve versions of this
classic dip. An Armenian version, known as *babaghanouj*,
adds green pepper and pomegranate seeds, shown as
options below.**

SERVES 6

- ◆ 1 kg/2 lb aubergines, trimmed and halved lengthways
- ◆ salt and freshly ground black pepper
- ◆ 50 ml/4 tbsp olive oil
- ◆ 5 spring onions, trimmed and finely chopped
- ◆ 1 green sweet pepper, cored, seeded and chopped (optional)
- ◆ 2 cloves garlic, crushed and finely chopped
- ◆ 2 ripe tomatoes, skinned, seeded and chopped
- ◆ pinch of cayenne pepper
- ◆ 15 ml/1 tbsp fresh lemon juice
- ◆ 3 tbsp finely chopped fresh coriander or parsley
- ◆ seeds from 1 pomegranate (optional)

Slash the aubergines on the sides and sprinkle with salt all
over. Place in a colander and let them drain for 30 minutes.
Rinse the aubergines and pat them dry with absorbent
kitchen paper.

Preheat the oven to 190°C/375°F/Gas mark 5. Place the
aubergines on a baking tray, cut side down, and brush all over
with oil. Bake in the oven for 40 minutes, until very tender.
Remove from the oven to cool.

Meanwhile, place 30 ml/2 tbsp olive oil in a frying pan. Add
the spring onions and the green pepper if used and stir for
5 minutes until soft. Add the garlic and cook for another
minute.

When the aubergine is cool, scrape out the flesh and chop it
finely. Add the rest of the oil to the pan and stir in the
chopped aubergine, together with the tomatoes, cayenne
pepper and seasoning to taste. Turn the heat to high and
bring the mixture to boiling point, mashing and stirring it at
the same time. Cover, lower the heat and simmer, stirring
occasionally, for about 30 minutes, or until the mixture has
thickened and most of the moisture has evaporated. Stir in
the lemon juice and coriander (substitute parsley and add the
pomegranate seeds if making *babaghanouj*), adjust the
seasoning and transfer the mixture to a bowl to cool. Leave to
stand for at least 3 hours; serve at room temperature. (The
caviar may be kept, chilled, for up to 3 days.)

TRANSCAUCASIAN CABBAGE AND MINT SALAD

TRANSCARKAZSKY SALAT IZ KAPUSTY Z MYATOY

◆ ◆ ◆

**Cabbage is a staple of the former Soviet Union, but
in the south the spicing is notably different, and sour cream
gives way to yoghurt, when used. This is a cool, refreshing
'coleslaw' served as a *zakuska* or to accompany a
picnic or outdoor meal.**

SERVES 6–8

- ◆ 23 ml/1½ tbsp lemon juice
- ◆ 30 ml/2 tbsp white wine vinegar
- ◆ 23 ml/1½ tbsp sunflower or olive oil
- ◆ ½ tsp sugar
- ◆ freshly ground black pepper
- ◆ 1 large red onion
- ◆ 1.25 kg/2½ lb white Dutch cabbage, outer leaves removed, cored, quartered and finely shredded
- ◆ 6 tbsp finely shredded fresh mint leaves

Beat together the lemon juice and vinegar in a large bowl.
Whisk in the oil, sugar and a generous dash of pepper. Halve
and finely slice all but one-quarter of the red onion. Stir the
onion slices into the dressing and wrap the remaining section
in aluminium foil. Then gently toss the shredded cabbage and
mint leaves in the dressing. Combine thoroughly and chill for
at least 3 hours.

Just before serving, slice the reserved onion and sprinkle
over the salad.

FISH

SEVAN LAKE TROUT YEREVAN-STYLE
SEVANSKAYA FOREL PO-YEREVANSKY

◆ ◆ ◆

Said to be the most delicious in Armenia, Sevan Lake trout can sometimes be found in the market at Yerevan, 70 km/46 miles to the southwest of the lake. The capital's market is richer in vegetables and herbs than is the norm. This recipe combines the flavours of that region, though we cannot duplicate the unique lake fish.

SERVES 4

- 4 375 g/12 oz brown or rainbow trout, cleaned and gutted
- salt and freshly ground black pepper
- 50 g/2 oz unsalted butter
- 225 g/8 oz bottled artichoke hearts in oil
- 50 g/2 oz plain flour
- 150 ml/¹/₄ pt fresh lemon juice
- 225 ml/8 fl oz water
- 75 ml 3 fl oz vegetable oil
- 23 ml/1¹/₂ tbsp dry white wine
- 3 tbsp drained capers
- 3 tbsp finely chopped fresh flat-leaved parsley
- pinch of sweet paprika
- small pinch of cayenne pepper

Rinse the trout and pat it dry with absorbent kitchen paper. Season to taste and set aside.

In a heavy saucepan over low heat, gently melt the butter until the solids have sunk to the bottom of the pan. Slowly pour off the clarified butter on the top and set aside. Discard the white residue and wash the pan.

Pour the oil from the bottled artichokes into the saucepan. Add 1 tsp flour and heat over a medium flame, stirring. Slowly add half the lemon juice and the water and bring the liquid to the boil, whisking. Lower the heat to simmer, stir in the artichoke hearts and cook, uncovered, for about 10 minutes, or until the sauce is reduced and thickened. Set aside.

Preheat the oven to 190°C/375°F/Gas Mark 5. Dredge the trout in flour and shake off the excess. Heat half the oil in a frying pan, and brown two of the trout on one side only. Remove to a roasting tin lined with oiled foil, add the rest of the oil to the frying pan and brown the two remaining trout on one side. Transfer to the roasting tin. Bake the trout for 10 minutes, or until the flesh is opaque and just beginning to flake. Carefully fillet the trout, arrange on four warmed serving plates, and sprinkle the fillets with the wine.

Stir the remaining lemon juice, the clarified butter and the capers into the sauce and heat through. Spoon the mixture over the fillets and sprinkle with the chopped parsley and the spices. Serve immediately.

GEORGIAN LAMB CUBES ON SKEWERS

SHASHLYK

◆ ◆ ◆

Shashlyk is the Georgian name for what is more commonly known here by its Turkish title, *shish kebab*. Unlike the Muslims, however, the Orthodox Georgians marinate their lamb in their dry Telliani wine.

SERVES 6

- ◆ *1 onion, chopped*
- ◆ *50 ml/2 fl oz mixed olive oil and vegetable oil*
- ◆ *1 bay leaf*
- ◆ *1 clove garlic, crushed*
- ◆ *2 tbsp finely chopped flat-leaved parsley*
- ◆ *1 tsp dried oregano*
- ◆ *$\frac{1}{4}$ tsp freshly ground black pepper*
- ◆ *large pinch cayenne pepper*
- ◆ *225 ml/8 fl oz dry red wine*
- ◆ *1 kg/2 lb lean boneless leg of lamb steak, cubed*
- ◆ *30 small white onions, peeled*
- ◆ *2 small red sweet peppers, cored, seeded and cut into square pieces*

Place the onion, oils, bay leaf, garlic, parsley, oregano, pepper and cayenne pepper in a thick plastic bag. Pour in the wine.

PHEASANT GEORGIAN-STYLE

PHAZAN PO-GRUZINSKY

◆ ◆ ◆

This dish is a relative of Walnut Chicken but has its own special accents. Made in its home region it would use sweet golden Gurdzhanni wine, but Madeira or *oloroso* sherry are acceptable substitutes.

SERVES 4

- ◆ *175 ml/6 fl oz boiling water*
- ◆ *1 heaped tsp Turkish or other green tea leaves*
- ◆ *675 g/1½ lb green grapes, stems removed*
- ◆ *1.25–1.5 kg/2½–3 lb pheasant, cleaned and trussed*
- ◆ *juice of 3 oranges*
- ◆ *1 tsp grated orange rind*
- ◆ *50 g/2 oz walnuts, chopped*
- ◆ *225 ml/8 fl oz Madeira*
- ◆ *salt and freshly ground black pepper*
- ◆ *45 g/1½ oz butter*
- ◆ *100 ml/4 fl oz game consommé*
- ◆ *quince jelly (optional)*

Pour the boiling water over the tea and allow it to steep for 10 minutes, then strain. Set aside the liquid tea and discard the leaves.

In a large bowl, mash the grapes with a potato masher or pestle. Continue until they are a pulpy mass and there is plenty of juice. Strain the mixture, discard the pulp and set aside the juice.

Place the pheasant in a Dutch oven or roasting tin with the orange rind and walnuts. Mix together the tea, grape juice, orange juice and Madeira and pour over the pheasant. Season to taste and dot the bird with butter. Cover with a lid or foil and bring the braising liquid to the boil on top of the stove. Reduce the heat and simmer for 45–50 minutes.

Preheat the oven to 220°C/425°F/Gas Mark 7. Lift out the pheasant and place it on a dish to drain. Strain the cooking liquid into a saucepan and discard the solids. Place the saucepan over medium-high heat and reduce until it is thick and syrupy, about 8 minutes. Carve the bird into serving pieces and return to the roasting tin. Cook uncovered for 20 minutes, or until it has browned lightly.

Transfer the pheasant to a serving dish. Pour the reduced stock over the pieces and serve immediately. Serve accompanied by a bowl of quince jelly, if available.

Hold tightly shut and shake vigorously to combine. Add the cubed lamb, tie the bag closed and place it in a bowl large enough to contain it comfortably. Leave for 24–36 hours in the refrigerator to mature.

Drain the lamb well but reserve the marinade. Thread the pieces on to 6 long skewers, alternating with the onions and red pepper.

Prepare the coals of a barbecue or preheat a grill. When ready, lay the skewers about 13 cm/5 in from the heat. Cook, turning once or twice and basting frequently, for about 10 minutes, or until the lamb is still pink inside but well browned. Serve with rice and Baku Tomato Preserve .

ARMENIAN CHICKEN AND CHICKPEA STEW

TYSHYONY TSYPLYONOK Z GRUSHAMI PO-ARMYANSKY

The Armenians have a spicy condiment sold as Aintab Red Pepper here in the West. Since it is difficult to find, two thin medium-hot red peppers have been substituted here.

SERVES 6

- 4 threads saffron
- 90 ml/3½ fl oz hot water
- 10 cloves garlic, crushed
- 2 fresh thin medium-hot red peppers, seeded and chopped
- 60 ml/4 tbsp vegetable or sunflower oil
- 1.5 kg/3 lb chicken breasts and thighs, washed and dried
- salt and freshly ground black pepper
- 2 tbsp ground coriander
- 1 tsp dried oregano
- 2 x 400 g/14 oz cans plum tomatoes, drained
- 425 ml/¾ pt water
- 575 g/1¼ lb can chickpeas, drained
- 30 ml/2 tbsp lemon juice

Soak the saffron in hot water for 10 minutes. Place the saffron and liquid, garlic and peppers in a blender or food processor. Process until finely chopped and set aside.

Heat the oil in a casserole over medium-hot heat. Season the chicken to taste and saute in batches until lightly browned. Remove to a plate and keep warm.

Reduce the heat and add the garlic puree. Stir with a wooden spoon for 2 minutes, then add the ground coriander and oregano. Stir for a further 2 minutes, then add the tomatoes. Break them up with the spoon while cooking for 3 minutes, then add the water. Add the chicken pieces and spoon the sauce over them. Bring to the boil, cover, and simmer over low heat for 20 minutes.

Add the chickpeas and continue to cook, covered, for a further 15 minutes. Remove the lid, stir in the lemon juice and increase the heat. Boil for 5 minutes to reduce the sauce. Serve immediately.

GEORGIAN MEAT AND TOMATO STEW
CHAKHOBILI

◆ ◆ ◆

This traditional dish is made as frequently with chicken as it is with lamb. In the old manner, it is cooked in a large iron pot over hot coals, but this version has been adapted to suit the modern hob.

SERVES 6

◆ 15 ml/1 tbsp vegetable or olive oil

◆ 1 kg/2 lb lamb steaks, trimmed of fat and cubed

◆ 2 onions, chopped

◆ 675 g/1¹/₂ lb whole Roma or plum tomatoes, skinned, seeded and roughly chopped

◆ 3 large potatoes, peeled and roughly cubed

◆ salt and freshly ground black pepper

◆ 50 g/2 oz fresh coriander, chopped

◆ 50 g/2 oz fresh flat-leaved parsley, chopped

◆ 5 fresh basil leaves, chopped

◆ 8 cloves garlic, crushed

Heat the oil in a large enamelled or stainless steel casserole until very hot but not smoking. Tilt to cover the bottom with the oil. Add the lamb pieces and brown, stirring with a wooden spoon, for 10 minutes. When the meat is coloured, add the onions and continue to stir until they are soft. Add the tomatoes and use the spoon to crush them. Stir in the potatoes and seasoning to taste. Cover and simmer over low heat for about 45 minutes or until the meat and potatoes are tender and the tomatoes have become a mushy sauce. Uncover and turn up the heat., Stir in the herbs and garlic and continue to stir as the sauce bubbles for 10 minutes. Take off the heat, cover, and leave to stand for 5–8 minutes before serving.

MELON AND WALNUT COMPOTE

KOMPOT IZ DYNI I OREKHOV

◆ ◆ ◆

**Versions of this simple dessert are eaten from
Greece through Georgia and Armenia to Uzbekistan.**

SERVES 6–8

◆ *2 small cantaloupe or
honeydew melons, halved,
seeded and cubed*

◆ *350 ml/12 fl oz honey*
◆ *350 g/12 oz walnuts,
chopped*

Place the melon cubes, with any juice, in a bowl. Add the
honey and toss to coat lightly. Stir in the walnuts. Divide the
mixture between individual bowls.

KAZAKHSTAN LAMB POTATO CAKES
KARTOPHELNYE PIROSHKI Z BARANINOY PO-KAZAKHSKY

◆ ◆ ◆

There are echoes of Afghan and Pakistani cooking in these spicy potato cakes, which resemble *pakhoras*. They would be served with *kumys* (mare's milk yoghurt, though today made commercially with cow's milk) in their native land.

MAKES 12

- ◆ 3 medium-sized red potatoes, peeled
- ◆ 1 onion
- ◆ 5 large eggs
- ◆ 350 g/12 oz lean minced lamb
- ◆ 3 tbsp plain flour
- ◆ 1 tbsp finely chopped flat-leaved parsley
- ◆ 1 tbsp finely chopped coriander
- ◆ 1/4 tsp ground cumin
- ◆ salt and freshly ground black pepper
- ◆ 25 g/1 oz clarified butter

Grate the potatoes on to a tea towel placed on a work surface. Twist the towel to squeeze out as much liquid as possible from the potatoes. Complete squeezing with your hands, then put the potatoes into a large bowl. Grate the onion into the bowl, and beat in the eggs, one at a time. Stir in the lamb, flour, parsley, coriander, cumin and seasoning to taste.

Melt the butter in a large frying pan over medium-high heat. Add the lamb and potato mixture in amounts of 3–4 tbsp spreading the cakes with the back of a spatula.

Cook until golden-brown, about 6 minutes a side. Drain on absorbent kitchen paper and keep warm until all the cakes have been cooked.

DEEP-FRIED HERB AND EGG ENVELOPES
GUTAP

◆ ◆ ◆

The dividing line between *samsa*, *gutap* and *beliashi* is a slim one, since they are all pastry cases containing many of the same fillings. *Samsas* can be either baked or deep-fried, while *beliashi* are shallow-fried and *gutap* are deep-fried. Here the fresh herbs usual to the latter are enveloped in a melting custard.

MAKES ABOUT 32

- ◆ 8 large eggs
- ◆ salt and freshly ground black pepper
- ◆ 45 g/1 1/2 oz unsalted butter, melted
- ◆ 1 tsp plain flour
- ◆ 100 g/4 oz fresh parsley, finely chopped
- ◆ 50 g/2 oz fresh dill, finely chopped
- ◆ 25 g/1 oz fresh coriander, finely chopped
- ◆ 50 g/4 oz kale, finely chopped
- ◆ 100 g/4 oz spring onions, finely chopped
- ◆ vegetable oil

For the dough

- ◆ 175 g/6 oz plain flour
- ◆ 150–175 g/5–6 fl oz lukewarm water
- ◆ salt
- ◆ 50 g/2 oz unsalted butter, softened

Beat the eggs in a large bowl and season to taste. Beat in the melted butter and the flour. Stir in the herbs, kale and spring onions.

Preheat the oven to 180°C/350°F/Gas Mark 4. Butter a baking dish or tin generously and pour in the egg mixture.

Bake in the oven for about 18 minutes, until the custard is just set. Remove from the oven and leave to cool to room temperature.

To make the dough, sift the flour into a bowl and make a well in the centre. Pour in the water, a good pinch of salt and half the butter and, using a plastic spoon or spatula, slowly stir the flour into the wet ingredients until well mixed. Then beat until it becomes a firm dough.

Transfer the dough to a floured surface and divide in half. Cover one half and set aside. Roll the other half into a rectangle, as thin as possible, and fold over once, then over again, until it is four layers thick. Roll out again as thinly as possible, and trim to about 23 x 20 cm/9 x 8 in. Cut the dough into 4 strips lengthways, then divide each strip into 4 equal squares.

Spoon a heaped tsp custard on to each square and draw up the corners to form a packet. Moisten your fingers and pinch the top to seal. Repeat with the remaining 15 or so squares. Cover with a damp cloth and set aside. Roll out the remaining pastry and repeat the process.

Fill a large saucepan or deep-fryer about 10–13 cm/4–5 in deep with oil. Heat until it is very hot (but not smoking) and spits when water is dropped into it (about 190°C/375°F). Fry the *gutap* in 3 batches for about 3–4 minutes each, turning, until they are golden and crisp. Drain on absorbent kitchen paper. Serve warm.

STEAMED LAMB DUMPLINGS
MANTY

◆ ◆ ◆

These are a speciality of Uzbekistan, and bear a resemblance to Mongolian pot-stickers and similar Chinese dumplings. The filling is often just minced lamb, but this version is tastier. *Manty* should be eaten with the fingers.

MAKES ABOUT 24

- *675 g/1½ lb minced lean lamb*
- *2 small onions, finely chopped*
- *45 ml/3 tbsp lemon juice*
- *50 g/2 oz raisins*
- *3 tbsp finely chopped mint*
- *¼ tsp ground cinnamon*
- *large pinch of cayenne pepper*

- *salt and freshly ground black pepper*
- *450 g/1 lb plain flour*
- *425 ml/¾ pt water*
- *butter*
- *225 ml/8 fl oz Greek- or Bulgarian-style*
- *yoghurt or 100 ml/4fl oz white wine vinegar (optional)*

In a large bowl, combine all of the ingredients except for the flour, water, butter and yoghurt or vinegar. Transfer half the mixture to the bowl of a food processor fitted with the metal blade. Process until of a pasty consistency. Set aside and process the remaining mixture. Combine the two meat mixtures.

Sift the flour into a large bowl. Make a well in the centre and pour in the water. Turn in the flour and mix thoroughly to make a smooth dough. Halve the dough, leave one half covered in the bowl and transfer the rest to a floured surface. Roll out thinly into a large rectangle.

Using a biscuit cutter or a wide-mouthed jar, cut out 12 cm/4½ in rounds. Place a scant 2 tbsp filling in the centre of each dough round. Top each with a dot of butter and pull up the sides of the dough over the filling to make a small purse. Moisten your fingers with water, then twist and pinch the top of each purse to close tightly. Set aside the prepared *manty*, covered with a damp cloth, and repeat the process with the remaining dough and filling.

Add water to a depth of 2.5–5 cm/1–2 in to a large saucepan and bring it to the boil. Place a steamer or colander over the boiling water, add half the *manty*, cover, and lower the heat so the water just simmers. Steam the *manty* for 15 minutes. Repeat with the remaining *manty*. Serve each batch as soon as it is cooked, together with a bowl of yoghurt or a small ramekin of vinegar for dipping, if desired.

STEAK TARTARE

MYASO PO-TATARSKY

◆ ◆ ◆

According to legend, Steak Tartare – the most renowned dish to come out Kazakhstan – was discovered by the fabled horsemen-warriors of Tartary. Always on the warpath, and with little or no time to cook their food, they tenderized meat under their saddles to make it palatable raw. In expensive Russian and East European restaurants, Steak Tartare is always a first course; in the West it is usually served as the entrée.

SERVES 4

- *2 large egg yolks*
- *3 spring onions, finely chopped*
- *10 ml/2 tsp Dijon-style mustard*
- *15 ml/1 tbsp Worcestershire sauce*
- *15 ml/1 tbsp bottled horseradish sauce*
- *15 ml/1 tbsp vegetable oil*
- *10 ml/2 tsp pepper vodka*
- *1 tbsp finely chopped capers*
- *450 g/1 lb fillet of beef, minced three times*
- *salt and freshly ground black pepper*

To garnish

- *watercress sprigs*
- *radishes, trimmed and scrubbed*
- *spring onions, trimmed*

Beat the eggs in a large bowl. One after the other, stir in the onions, mustard, Worcestershire sauce, horseradish, oil, vodka and capers. With your hands, gently work the beef into the mixture, and season to taste. Form into 4 patties and arrange on a serving dish. Garnish attractively with the watercress, radishes and spring onions.

ZAKUSKI

BAKED PASTIES

SAMSA

◆ ◆ ◆

**These baked *samsa* bear a distinct resemblance to
the more northerly *pierogi*, though the spicing is
unmistakeably Asian. They make delicious hors d'oeuvres
for a drinks party – as do all Central Asian pastries,
dumplings and fritters.**

MAKES ABOUT 40

- ◆ *450 g/1 lb lean minced beef*
- ◆ *2 small onions, chopped*
- ◆ *salt and freshly ground black pepper*
- ◆ *pinch of cayenne pepper*
- ◆ *50 g/2 oz fresh parsley, chopped*
- ◆ *50 g/2 oz fresh coriander, chopped*
- ◆ *45 g/1½ oz toasted pine nuts*

For the dough

- ◆ *225 g/8 oz unsalted butter, softened*
- ◆ *225 ml/8 fl oz Greek- or Bulgarian-style yoghurt*
- ◆ *275–300 g/10–11 oz plain flour*
- ◆ *1 heaped tsp salt*
- ◆ *1 egg*
- ◆ *15 ml/1 tbsp water*

Make the dough first. Cream the butter with the yoghurt in a large bowl. Slowly sift in the flour, a little at a time, beating it in after each addition. Add the salt at the same time. Continue until you have used up all but 1–2 tbsp of the flour. If the dough is still tacky, add as much of the remaining flour as is necessary to make it firm. Cover with cling film and chill for 3–5 hours.

Meanwhile, make the filling. Place the meat, onions, seasoning to taste, cayenne pepper, parsley and coriander in the bowl of a food processor fitted with the metal blade. Process until it is of a pasty consistency. Remove to a bowl and work in the toasted pine-nuts. Chill until needed.

On a floured surface, roll out the dough into a large rectangle. With a biscuit cutter or lid, cut out 7.5–9 cm/3–3½ in circles. Spoon a heaped tsp filling on each circle, moisten the edges and fold over the dough to make a crescent. Use the prongs of a fork to press and crimp the edges of the crescents. Arrange the pasties on an oiled baking sheet and chill for 30 minutes.

Preheat the oven to 200°C/400°F/Gas Mark 6. Make an egg wash by beating the egg with the water and brush over the pasties. Bake them for about 15 minutes, until golden-brown.

POULTRY & MEAT

UZBEKISTAN GRILLED QUAIL OR PARTRIDGE

PYEREPYOL ILI KUROPATKA-GRILL PO-UZBEKSKI

◆ ◆ ◆

**Though Uzbekistan is largely desert it also contains
the foothills of the Tian Shan and Alay mountain ranges,
in which can be found plentiful game. Grilled quail and
partridge are a speciality, first marinated in spices
and thick cream**

SERVES 4

- ◆ *8 quail or 4 small partridges, cleaned and gutted, heads removed*
- ◆ *90 ml/6 tbsp fresh lemon juice*
- ◆ *salt and freshly ground black pepper*
- ◆ *2 cloves garlic, crushed and finely chopped*
- ◆ *2 tsp peeled and grated fresh root ginger*
- ◆ *½ tsp allspice*
- ◆ *½ tsp nutmeg*
- ◆ *150 ml/¼ pt double cream*
- ◆ *vegetable oil*

If using partridge, cut them in half. Place the whole quail or halved partridges in a wide bowl and sprinkle with the lemon juice and a heaped tsp salt. Toss and rub the birds with your hands, and leave them to marinate for 1 hour. Then add the remaining ingredients except for the oil, toss, and chill the mixture for 3–4 hours, moving the pieces around once or twice.

Prepare the coals of a barbecue or preheat a grill. On each of four metal skewers, either thread 2 quail or 2 halves of partridge. Truss the birds on, if necessary. Brush the birds with oil and lay them about 10 cm/4 in above the hot coals or under the grill. Cook for about 20–25 minutes, turning once or twice, until the birds are just cooked through and nicely browned. Serve immediately.

POULTRY & MEAT

ALMA-ATA PILAF

ALMA-ATA PLOV

◆ ◆ ◆

**There are numerous *plov* recipes originating in
Central Asia; this one from the capital of Kazakhstan
utilizes the rich bounty of fruit which grow there –
the apples are particularly famous.**

SERVES 6

◆ *50 g/2 oz blanched slivered
  almonds*
◆ *50 ml/4 tbsp vegetable oil*
◆ *450 g/1 lb lamb steaks,
  cubed*
◆ *2 large carrots, cut into
  julienne strips*
◆ *2 large onions, thinly sliced*
◆ *75 g/3 oz dried apricots,
  chopped*
◆ *50 g/2 oz raisins*

◆ *675 g/1¹/₂ lb long-
  grained white rice*
◆ *salt and freshly ground
  black pepper*
◆ *425 ml/³/₄ pt chicken
  stock*
◆ *150 ml/¹/₄ pt orange juice*
◆ *1 tsp grated orange rind*
◆ *600 ml/1 pt water*
◆ *1 medium red apple,
  cored and chopped*

Preheat the oven to 200°C/400°F/Gas Mark 6. Scatter the
almonds on a baking sheet and toast in the oven until golden,
about 5 minutes. Set aside and turn the oven down to
180°C/350°F/Gas Mark 4.

Heat the oil in a large frying pan over medium-high heat.
When just smoking, add the lamb cubes and sauté for
6 minutes, or until well browned. Transfer the meat with a
slotted spoon to a large casserole.

Turn the heat down slightly and sauté the carrots in the oil
for 3 minutes, stirring, then add the onions and continue to
sauté for another 6 minutes, until the onions are soft and
lightly coloured. Stir in the dried apricots, raisins and rice.
Cook for 2 minutes until the rice is coated with the oil and is
becoming opaque.

Add the rice mixture to the casserole with the meat. Season
to taste, then pour over the chicken stock, orange juice and
rind, and water. Bring to the boil, then cover the casserole
and transfer it to the oven. Bake for 40 minutes, or until all
the liquid is absorbed.

Remove the *plov* from the oven, stir in the chopped apple,
and transfer it to a large serving dish, making a neat mound.
Scatter the toasted almonds over the top and serve.

UZBEKISTAN SWEET WALNUT BRITTLE

SLADKOYE PYECHENYE IZ GRYETSKIKH OREKHOV PO UZBEKSKY

◆ ◆ ◆

The Central Asians are famous for their sweet tooth – and for their love of nuts. In this dish the two make a perfect marriage, bound by the sweetened evaporated milk common in their desserts.

MAKES ABOUT 700G/1¹/₂ LB

- 225 ml/8 oz light brown sugar
- ¹/₂ tsp ground cinnamon
- ¹/₄ tsp ground allspice
- ¹/₄ tsp ground ginger
- 75 ml/3 fl oz evaporated milk
- 350 g/12 oz walnuts
- ¹/₂ tsp vanilla essence

Place the sugar, cinnamon, allspice, ginger and evaporated milk in a heavy saucepan and stir over high heat for about 5 minutes, or until the sugar dissolves and the mixture reaches soft ball stage (115°C/238°F on a sugar thermometer.)

Remove the pan from the heat and stir in the nuts and vanilla essence. Make sure all the nuts are coated, then pour out on to a sheet of greaseproof paper. Allow to cool, then break into chunks. Store in an airtight container.